ple are saying about

image in Japan

A Zen master once asked a disciple, "What is the purpose of your pilgrimage?" The student answered, "I don't know." The master approved, saying, "Not knowing is most intimate." In Joan Stamm's account of her indomitable trek to 33 Japanese Buddhist temples, we encounter the intimate heart of Buddhism: fearless compassion. Through vivid observations and clear insights, she invites readers to realize the great compassionate spirit abiding within each of us.
Karen Maezen Miller, author of *Paradise in Plain Sight: Lessons from a Zen Garden*

This deeply observed and exquisitely written journey is filled with Zen wisdom and mystery that awakens the reader to the hunger of search that simmers within us. Joan Stamm's spiritual experience fulfills the four aspects of pilgrimage: seeing into one's heart, training the mind through meditation, being gladdened in the journey, and transforming one's daily life. Take this pilgrimage with her and discover for yourself the transmission of Kannon's lived compassion in all its myriad forms. It's a gift, intensely human and fulfilling, a treasure not to be missed.
Eido Frances Carney Roshi, Abbess and Teacher, Olympia Zen Center and author of *Kakurenbo: Or the Whereabouts of Zen Priest Ryokan*

Ms Joan Stamm has written a delightful and engaging narrative of her experiences on Japan's ages old Saikoku pilgrimage to thirty-three temples devoted to the worship of the Bodhisattva of Compassion and Mercy, Kannon. Weaving together both her knowledge of Buddhism and of Japanese culture, and her experiences first with the people she meets along the way and then at the temples themselves, Ms Stamm has given readers an eloquent tapestry they are sure to enjoy.

Nicholas Teele, author and co-translator of *Ono No Komachi: Poems, Stories, No Plays* and other works.

An excellent, fully personalized, and well-informed account of Japan's oldest circulatory Buddhist pilgrimage.

Michael Pye, Professor of Religion (emeritus), University of Marburg, Germany and author of *Japanese Buddhist Pilgrimage*.

Joan D. Stamm is the author of *Heaven and Earth are Flowers: Reflections on Ikebana and Buddhism*. Boston, Wisdom Publications, 2010.

A Pilgrimage in Japan

The 33 Temples of Kannon

A Pilgrimage
in Japan

The 33 Temples of Kannon

Joan D. Stamm

**MANTRA
BOOKS**

Winchester, UK
Washington, USA

First published by Mantra Books, 2018
Mantra Books is an imprint of John Hunt Publishing Ltd., Laurel House, Station Approach,
Alresford, Hants, SO24 9JH, UK
office1@jhpbooks.net
www.johnhuntpublishing.com
www.mantra-books.net

For distributor details and how to order please visit the 'Ordering' section on our website.

Text copyright: Joan D. Stamm 2017

ISBN: 978 1 78535 750 3
978 1 78535 751 0 (ebook)
Library of Congress Control Number: 2017944447

A CIP catalogue record for this book is available from the British Library.

Design: Stuart Davies

Printed and bound by CPI Group (UK) Ltd, Croydon, CR0 4YY, UK

We operate a distinctive and ethical publishing philosophy in
all areas of our business, from our global network of authors to
production and worldwide distribution.

Contents

To my sister Gwen who completed the pilgrimage
with me.

Permissions and Credits

Authorship of the *goeikas*, or song-poems, chanted at each Kannon temple is traditionally attributed to Emperor Kazan who reigned in the 10th century. However recent scholarship has revealed that the original authors may have been pilgrims or founding priests, of whose names have been lost to antiquity.

Translations of the goeikas for temple 1-4, 6-24 & 26-29 are the result of collaboration between Cate Kodo Juno and Nicholas Teele, and appear with their permission.

Translation of the goeika for temple 5 is credited to Michael Pye, and appears with his permission.

Translations of the goeikas for temple 25 and 30-33 are credited solely to Nicholas Teele with his permission.

Haiku by Santoka Teneda is credited as follows: Santoka Teneda, haiku from *Mountain Tasting: Haiku and Journals of Santoka Teneda*, translated by John Stevens. Translation copyright © 1980, 2009 by John Stevens. Reprinted with the permission of The Permissions Company, Inc., on behalf of White Pine Press.

Abbreviated versions of "Kami Daigoji – Temple 11," and "Tsubosakadera – Temple 6," originally appeared in Romar Traveler Magazine as "Hiking in the Land of Yamabushi: A Journey to Mt. Daigo, Japan," and "The Big Buddhas of Japan: Tsubosakadera," respectively.

Acknowledgments

First, and foremost, a loving bow of gratitude to my sister and fellow pilgrim, Gwen Stamm. Without her steady companionship I would not have ventured to the remote Kannon pilgrim sites of Japan. She provided wit, humor and encouragement every step of the way. Her friendship and mutual love for Japan is truly a blessing.

A big thank you to my sister Carollyne Coby and brother-in-law Dennis Fill who helped finance all three trips. Their generosity has made so many things possible.

I am ever so grateful to Ed Readicker-Henderson who wrote *The Traveler's Guide to Japanese Pilgrimages* over 20 years ago. His guide to the 33 temples of Kannon made our pilgrimage possible.

A round of applause goes to Cate Kodo Juno for her beautiful and invaluable website (sacredjapan) on the Kannon pilgrimage. She has brought another dimension of the pilgrimage to the English-speaking world by providing a deeper layer of understanding to the legends, icons, history, and points of interest of each temple. She also offered assistance on directions for Part II of our journey which proved to be invaluable. Kodo and Readicker-Henderson have paved the way for all of us.

A bow to Nicholas Teele and Michael Pye, pilgrim scholars and translators, who offered their assistance and knowledge of the goeikas (song-poems) that accompany each temple.

I will always have a special heart of gratitude for Hiro Kitagami who volunteered to personally escort us to three of the temples (one a distant mountain hike) with offers to help us with the entire route if need be; and to his fellow English club friend, Junko Nakaura, who graciously welcomed us to Wakayama City and assisted Hiro-san with our visit to Temple 2, Kimiidera.

A big thank you also goes to Shosaku Ito who made our stay

in Kokawa and our visit to Temple 3, Kokadera, most memorable; and to his English club friends who delighted and charmed us over dinner.

A bow to all the Japanese people who helped us along the way; although I don't know your names, I will always remember your kindness.

My very deep gratitude goes out to all my Buddhist teachers who exemplify Kannon's wisdom and compassion and inspire me to continue on the path. Without the many translators, writers, and teachers of Buddhism, the dharma would remain inaccessible.

And lastly, the deepest bow goes to Buddha Shakyamuni who realized Ultimate Truth over 2,500 hundred years ago so that we could become free of suffering and reach our own state of enlightenment; and of course to Kannon, the Bodhisattva of Compassion, whom we aspire to emulate.

A sincere bow and *gassho* to all!

Part I

Preface

More than one expert on global crises and the environment has suggested that changing "tourism" to "pilgrimage" would have a significant positive impact on the world. In other words, bringing "sacred intent" to travel, to the land, people and places we encounter when traveling, whether domestic or international, could transform the planet. In October of 2011, I heard that call to "pilgrimage"—a physical act of affirmation: of life, of spiritual awakening, and the positive potential to make a difference.

Inspired by the land and people of Japan since the early 1990s, when my sister Gwen and I had teaching jobs in Kobe, our pilgrimage would encompass seven prefectures, including a remote area of the Kii Peninsula, an island in the middle of Lake Biwa, and a journey to the Japan Sea. The Kannon Saigoku Thirty-three Temple Pilgrimage that honors the Bodhisattva of Compassion: Kannon (also known in Japan as Kannon-sama or Kanzeon; in China as Guanyin; and in India as Avalokiteshvara) was our pilgrimage of choice. Back then, in 2011, and even more so now, in 2017 as I finalize this preface, compassion: the ability to put ourselves in others' shoes, to feel another's suffering and engage in actions of loving-kindness competed globally with fear, hatred, and the negation of others. Could a pilgrimage of compassion make a difference?

Since I first saw images of Kannon over twenty-five years ago, I have been struck by the potential she held as a representative of female spirituality—even though "she" is sometimes a "he"—not found in any other Buddhist iconography. Because Kannon emanates such a strong aura of femininity, I think of her and relate to her—as do the Japanese and Chinese—as female, no matter which gender she's manifesting. Her icons, and therefore her unlimited nature, abound. She appears as Eleven-headed Kannon, Thousand-Armed, Horse-headed, White-robed, and many others. She is a protector, healer, companion, mother, purifier and an all-encompassing cosmic being. Like Tara, the Tibetan female *bodhisattva* of compassion, Kannon is known as "the one who hears the cries of the world." And in today's world those "cries" are on the rise, and intensifying. A physical journey of spiritual significance held the promise of creating deep imprints upon the mind, and of benefiting others if one had the proper motivation. Buddha himself recommended pilgrimage to holy places.

* * *

They say your pilgrimage begins the moment you make it your intention, and on that day in October, although nothing had been booked, we *had* made it our intention to do the pilgrimage the following November. Worries began to emerge. Would I have enough money? Would I be able to do the mountain hiking with my previous heart problems? Would my sister's injured ankle allow her to go up and down mountain slopes and uneven stone stairs? How would we get by outside the main urban areas with our limited Japanese?

On that day in autumn, the rather unexpected reassuring voice—the one that I now recognize as my inner Kannon—said, "Don't worry. Everything is going to be fine." The voice calmed me immediately. At that moment Worry Mind surrendered to Kannon Mind, the mind of quiet confidence, of faith in following the unique, and sometimes mysterious, twists and turns of one's personal journey. I recognized that day that my pilgrimage had indeed begun.

In the Lotus Sutra, a Mahayana teaching first written down approximately 2,000 years ago, Kannon, a.k.a. Avalokiteshvara, or Regarder of the Cries of the World Bodhisattva is said to appear in whatever form humans need: a woman, man, girl, boy, high official, ordinary citizen... the list goes on to name the thirty-three manifestations of Kannon. In Japan, Regarder of the Cries of the World Bodhisattva appeared as the bodhisattva Kannon; and to honor the symbolism of the Lotus Sutra and Kannon's thirty-three manifestations, Buddhist priests established many Kannon pilgrimages. The Saigoku Pilgrimage, the most beautiful and famous, still beckons, ten centuries later, to the spiritual wanderer; it still holds promise for healing and transformation. I, and millions of others, sought a direct connection with our own divine nature, our Buddha spirit or Christ consciousness. For this reason we traveled to Jerusalem, Mecca, Bodhgaya and the hinterlands of Japan where revelations, miracles, healings and transformations had been recorded for millennia.

In all of Kannon's various forms, her vow remains the same: to aid anyone and all in distress. My "distress" wasn't life threatening; it wasn't an incurable illness, or an inconsolable grief or loss. I wasn't going through a divorce, career shift, change of residence or any other "high stress" indicator. And yet, I felt restless and dissatisfied; sadness and a feeling of powerlessness had crept into my psyche over catastrophic world events. My experience was that of "*dukkha*" or Life is Suffering: Buddha's First Noble Truth, a teaching on the many aspects of "distress"— both subtle and not so subtle—that humans experience. Could a Kannon pilgrimage alleviate such a restrained but nagging kind of torment?

Contentment—the prescribed antidote—remained elusive, even while living on an idyllic island, as I did, in one of the most beautiful places in the country. Suffering could be quiet and persistent, a steady relentless feeling of something not quite right, of a life that hadn't been fully realized. And although my immediate environment remained peaceful, safe, and relatively harmonious, outside our protected island enclave the world at large grew more dangerous, heartless and polarized; it had recently exploded with fear, hatred and conflict.

With Kannon, the feminine aspect of spirituality maintained its powerful mythological heritage. The Bodhisattva of Compassion, depicted with strength and tenderness, unapologetic and confident, embodied our highest aspiration. What then could I learn from the divine manifestation of female divinity if I spent significant time and resources truly contemplating what she represented? What would I absorb from the temple sites where millions of other Kannon devotees had journeyed over the course of the last 1,000 years? In this climate of yearning and curiosity, of wanting world travel to be more than exotic entertainment, the idea of "pilgrimage" drew me into deeper realms.

Under the Asian zodiac, the intended year for our journey happened to be the Year of the Dragon—dragons being spiritual messengers, symbols of transformation, and defenders of Buddhism in Japan. Two-thousand twelve also marked the end of the Mayan calendar, prophesized as a time of "planetary shift" into higher consciousness. On a personal and mundane level, it was the year I turned 60. All things considered, 2012 seemed like an auspicious year to begin a pilgrimage. Along with these "cosmic" indicators and my own need for spiritual fulfillment, deteriorating world affairs played in the background like a funeral dirge. I needed to do something other than bear witness to endless wars and environmental ruin, to destructive foreign policy and corporate greed that put profit over everything else. Manifest suffering begged for a metaphysical antidote.

Ryozen Kannon, an 80-foot concrete and steel statue in Eastern Kyoto stood as a memorial to the millions of Japanese who had lost their lives in World War II. In 1991, when I first saw her serene smile looming above the trees, the U.S. had just completed its first assault on Iraq, a.k.a "Operation Desert Storm." We would go on to Bosnia, Afghanistan, and "Operation Iraqi Freedom." Today in 2017, we are still engaged in Iraq and Afghanistan, with new fronts in Syria: a once prosperous country that has been completely destroyed. Sixty-five million displaced people and refugees, the highest ever recorded, seek protection from war, poverty and famine. Oil drilling, spilling and fracking continue to threaten sacred sites, pristine lakes, rivers, wetlands, and waterways. Coal trains emitting toxic dust continue to lumber through the unspoiled corridors of the Pacific Northwest. Oil pipelines threaten clean water and sacred indigenous lands. Mass shootings in U.S. cities have become common place. Immigrants and refugees from Muslim countries live under the threat of being banned from a nation once respected for offering refuge. The most divisive presidential election in U.S. history has left half the country feeling denigrated, disempowered, fearful, and deeply depressed. Many are asking what will happen to the environment, to our health care, climate change policies, and laws that protect the rights of all citizens.

Kannon—and the Kannon in all of us—cries buckets of tears as we witness heartless cruelty, disrespect of others, disregard for the earth and the never ending destruction of animal species, wilderness and the purity of the natural environment.

At what point will human beings stop to consider the Buddhist precept "do no harm." What catastrophe will mark the tipping point to compel us to work for the good of all rather than special interests?

Faced with "suffering," internal, external and subliminal, I wondered if one person's pure intention could potentially have an impact. The answer seemed to lie in the realm of physics; simply stated, elevating individual consciousness fell into the realm of pebbles in ponds and the movement of butterfly wings rippling across the globe—actions create movement, and movement creates change. The law of cause and effect, or karma, would be put into motion, as it had for every pilgrim who has ever taken up pilgrimage.

For thousands of years, pilgrims have been depositing positive energy through prayers and aspirations at sacred sites, creating a treasure-house of "precious jewels." Thus, in the face of cynics who denounced pilgrimage as a superstitious pastime,

I trusted that my venture of time, money and commitment *would* have an affirmative outcome. Nothing is lost in the great world order of cause and effect.

The power of wisdom and compassion resides in every one of us. We, as carriers of Kannon's enlightened potential, are the stewards of the earth, the potential saviors of humankind, and the bearers of acts of compassion.

The intention to remain open to whatever Kannon—our own spark of Buddha consciousness—wished to reveal, teach or impart remained at the forefront. I would let the essence of each temple experience guide me toward a deeper understanding of the teachings of Buddha as expressed through the aspect of Kannon, all the while making prayers for world peace, planetary healing, spiritual evolution, and divine inspiration—the way all previous pilgrims had for centuries.

The reassuring voice that arose that day in October to dispel Worry Mind affirmed that a hidden river of possibility could be tapped. We, and the world at large, could be driven by the highest ideals rather than sink into greed, apathy, hatred or violence.

Namu Kanzeon Bosatsu! (I entrust myself to Kannon, the Bodhisattva of Compassion!)

Chapter 1

Preparing for Pilgrimage

It is often said that when you embark on any spiritual journey, whether it's a trip to meet your guru, to engage in retreat, or, in our case, to begin a spiritual pilgrimage, obstacles pop up to try and thwart your good intentions. By November 1st, 2012, the date of our flight to Japan, most of our obstacles had been waylaid except for one: an unexpected missed connection in San Francisco due to hurricane Sandy and the shortage of a flight crew.

Worry Mind, tested and re-tested, didn't easily give way to its higher sister. Anxiety would plague me at different stages along the pilgrimage. Still, confronting Worry Mind the previous year and its antidote Kannon Mind, would begin to dissipate the insidious wormy maneuvers of raw fear that seeped in now and then, even little anxieties about whether to begin with Temple 1 and proceed methodically from 1 to 33 (as recommended by pilgrim tours), or devise some other route that better fit our needs, circumstances and the ever changing fall weather in Japan. Did a consecutive route really matter?

Arriving a day later than planned, we opened to "guidance," and plotted our course. In one month's time our goal was to visit the first 19 temples, but not necessarily in consecutive order. In spring of 2014 we hoped to return to finish the remaining 14. (In reality, although we didn't know it at the time, we wouldn't complete our pilgrimage until October of 2015.)

So, where to begin?

Noting the words of Joseph Campbell who said, "Unless you leave room for serendipity, how can the divine enter in?", we followed an intuitive course and began at our home base, Kyoto; and one of the busiest and most beloved temples in all of Japan:

Kiyomizudera, Temple 16.

Like millions of pilgrims who had traveled the Saigoku route for the last 1,000 years, my prayers for global and personal healing would be left in the hands of Kannon—not as an act of powerlessness, but with the intention of filling those hands until they overflowed. Maybe all the world needed to set off a flood of positive change was one more heartfelt prayer.

With the feeling of being "the hundredth monkey," (the famous macaques observed by Japanese scientists in a moment of evolution) I heeded Kannon's whispering call to set sail into the uncharted waters of spiritual pilgrimage, hoping that her wise and compassionate guidance would bear delectable fruit.

But first things first, which meant partaking in our pre-pilgrimage ritual.

In *The Art of Pilgrimage*, by Phil Cousineau, he relates that, "All sacred journeys are marked by ritual ceremony." Our "ritual ceremony" took place at Shunkoin, a sub-temple of Myoshinji, the largest Zen temple complex in Kyoto. The head abbot offered morning *zazen* with a dharma talk, the perfect prelude to our Kannon pilgrimage.

Stone walkways that zigzagged from north to south and east to west transported us further into quiet interiors of Myoshinji with its myriad sub-temples, each one solemnly contained behind high walls. Open gates invited us to peek into hidden places, sanctuaries with white stones raked into wave like designs, black pines pruned into natural sculptures and autumn maples dropping scarlet leaves into placid ponds. All of Myoshinji, one vast compound of cultivated beauty, transfixed with the asymmetrical and minimalist aesthetic of Japanese gardens: peaceful designs that tended to induce immediate tranquility.

We came upon a small sign in English indicating arrival at our destination: Shunkoin, or Ray of Spring Light Temple. The stone path led us through the front gate and garden where, we learned later, D.T. Suzuki, the father of American Zen, had planted several azaleas in years past. Captivated by the impeccable landscape, we hesitated momentarily until warmly greeted by Rev. Takafumi Kawakami (or Taka) who appeared in his monk's *samue* (Zen meditation/work clothes). He had learned English in the States while attending college, and, as Japanese culture prescribes, returned to Japan to assume responsibility for the family temple. Not your ordinary Japanese abbot, Rev. Kawakami, per his website, openly advocates for equal rights of the LGBT community, advertises open marriage ceremonies and offers himself as "a bridge between East and West."

He led us down a long polished wood corridor into a tatami mat zendo, where he offered either a cushion or chair for our meditation. After one period of zazen—about twenty minutes or so of silent breath counting—Taka gave a dharma talk on the ordinary aspects of the Buddhist life. He insisted that Westerners not romanticize Buddhism or monastic life. He discouraged any impressions that Buddhist monasteries contained anything mysterious or exotic. On the contrary, he explained that Buddhism: the practice of engaging in ordinary life just as it is; contained nothing lofty or idealistic. Rev. Taka, a no nonsense kind of guy, struck a resonant cord, even though I had long since given up dreamy notions about monastic life. Later in the day, and many times after, I would be reminded of the importance of his down-to-earth teaching about "life as it is" versus my preconceived ideas of how life ought to be—how *pilgrimage* ought to be, or even how the world order "ought to be."

After zazen, he led us back to the waiting room for *wagashi* (a Japanese confection) and bowl of *matcha* (whisked powdered green tea). I felt calm, peaceful and inspired. Taka's teaching grounded me in the here and now of Buddhist practice, and set the proper mood for what lay ahead: the beginning of our "official" pilgrimage. We had been blessed through the simple practice of zazen, by receiving a Buddhist teaching and drinking a bowl of tea—a simple ritual imbued with the principles of "harmony, respect, purity and tranquility." We would repeat this centuries old ceremony of *Chado* many times throughout our pilgrimage.

After a relaxed and informal chat with our host and fellow guests, the time had come to leave this timeless inner sanctuary for the greater world that awaited us. Once we said our goodbyes and zigzagged back to the outer gate of Myoshinji, the serenity of our morning Zen experience soon faded into the task of figuring out bus, train and subway routes as we headed off in the direction of our first pilgrimage temple on the other side of the city. If Kannon had set up a test on keeping and maintaining a peaceful mind, we were about to fail.

Chapter 2

With the wind in the pines,
Cupping my hands to drink
The pure waters
Of the Otowa waterfall,
Brings coolness to my soul

Kiyomizudera – Temple 16

The Bodhisattva Birth Canal

Forced to confront a few disquieting thoughts about pilgrimage, namely that "temple" did not mean "quiet and contemplative," and "pilgrimage" did not always mean "a solitary journey of the soul," Kiyomizudera taught me that pilgrimage cannot be separated from life. Taka's dharma talk immediately became quite relevant. Buddhism emphasized that we should remain in the here and now without the overlay of judgment, expectation or preconceived notions. We had to "get it" the way "it" is.

As soon as we disembarked from our standing-room-only bus experience, followed the packs of tourists turning the corner into a narrow street, and observed the throngs making their way up Otowa Mountain toward our destination, the only attitude one could take and still have a positive experience was surrender. Before long, we landed at the foot of one of the most beloved temples in all of Japan: Pure Spring Temple. The name itself promised renewal.

I would soon learn that the power of pilgrimage resides not only in physical place, icons and rituals, but also in other pilgrims. If allowed to take in the various aspects of pilgrimage without judgment or resistance, the journey itself tended to induce a higher level of thinking, doing and intending. The vibrations, or life force (*ki* in Japanese) of sacred place and the actions or rituals performed there had been accumulating for centuries. In a still moment, without distraction, one felt this reservoir of spiritual power.

What we brought to each moment, to each action, was our intention, presence (or non-presence) our good or bad, positive or negative thoughts. This could be said for pilgrimage, daily life or world events. I imagined then—imagination being a powerful tool in a mob scene—a positive, exalted bubble of invisible energy enveloping each pilgrim as they entered the hallowed ground of Kiyomizudera, the temple dubbed "the spiritual heart and soul of Kyoto." Among the thousands of pilgrims who visited that day, some appeared to be truly devoted and reverent; others perhaps dazed, duty bound or slightly bored; still others— mostly school kids—giggly or goofy. This temple, *our* Temple #1 on the Saigoku Pilgrimage, had the effect of pilgrims on a conveyor belt—bodies moving by some unseen hand—resist and you'll have a stressful, rotten time; don't resist and you might enjoy being part of an international spiritual love fest.

Kiyomizudera reflected all of humanity: thousands of seekers jostling metaphorically through the gates of heaven and hell. The spirit of Kiyomizudera manifested the myriad aspects of "letting go"—of preconceived ideas and romantic notions; the desire for peace, silence or solitude; and later, when we traveled through Daizuigu Bodhisattva's birth canal, the letting go of certainty, sight, safety, and even clinging to one's own incarnate existence.

But I'm getting ahead of myself. First we needed to follow the pilgrim's etiquette and acquire the pilgrim's paraphernalia—the latter being one of the reasons for starting at Temple 16.

To gain a sense of orientation, we stopped at the *temizuya*, or purification basin to read up on "pilgrim etiquette." We had been so distracted by the swarms of school kids, hand-holding couples, senior bus tours, and other foreigners moving as one body up the steep stone stairs, that we lost certainty about whether we *had* crossed through the main gate, the traditional place where the pilgrim should bow in humble gratitude.

One glance at our "Places of Interest" guide told us that, yes, we had missed the main gate, the famous "Red Gate" or *Akamon*. In looking back at the masses still moving as one up the stone stairs, we decided to bow at some other strategic spot and proceeded with our purification ritual. By then the day's travel snags, delays and general irritations, had accumulated; we had a lot to purify.

As instructed, we filled the purification ladle with water that gurgled forth from a dragon's mouth, held it over the area *around* the basin (never *over* the basin), poured a little over one hand and then the other, saved enough to pour a bit into our cupped hand for a sip (never drink from the ladle itself), and used the remaining water to purify the ladle by tipping it vertically, allowing the rest of the water to run down the handle before placing it back. This ablution ritual, performed at all Buddhist temples and Shinto shrines in Japan, goes back to the days when pilgrims stood naked in ocean or river and purified their entire body. Luckily for us the ritual has been modified, but the intent of purifying thoughts, ill health, negative tendencies or disturbing emotions, is still the same. My mind always felt a little clearer, lighter and reverential after this purification rite.

Once we paid our fee and officially entered the temple complex, we performed our next bit of pilgrim etiquette: ringing the bell inside the *hondo* or main hall. Out of respect we removed our shoes and placed them next to the dozens of others lined up in rows along the base of the hondo platform. Now we were ready to step into the inner sanctuary.

At the toes of a ten-foot gold statue of Amida Buddha—the word "Amida" means "infinite or immeasurable light" and personifies Ultimate Truth or non-conceptual reality—pilgrims kneel on a flat brocade cushion to strike the giant bronze bowl. When it came my turn, I knelt down and struck it once. A Japanese woman standing in line immediately corrected me.

"Strike three times. Buddha, dharma, sangha."

Ah, of course. In the frenzy of it all I had already forgotten the three jewels of Buddhism. But over the course of the pilgrimage, I would get many more reminders and opportunities to honor the Awakened Mind, the Truth of the Teachings, and the Community of Practitioners. I corrected my mistake, moved out of the way for the next person, and stood under the giant statue trying to capture the beauty and essence of "Amida" in my camera.

A replica of the original Thousand-armed Eleven-headed Kannon could be viewed distantly in the back of the ornately gold tabernacle. Surprisingly few visitors ventured into this inner sanctuary to take a peek at Kannon or Amida Buddha, but I found the blackened walls and dim lighting of the hondo to be a quiet respite from the thousands of visitors milling about elsewhere. For at least a few moments, I had time to turn inward and make a few prayers for inner guidance. Kannon's symbolic thousand arms (in actuality 42) and thousand eyes testified to her ability to see and reach out in one thousand ways to heal, inspire and teach. Her eleven heads signified the stages of the bodhisattva path, with the 11th head being that of Amida Buddha, indicating that Kannon was an emanation, or a form appearing out of the formless in service to Amida, the Buddha of Infinite Light.

All the symbolic representations of the vast and complex teachings of Buddhism contained in this one inner sanctuary alone could be studied and contemplated for years; and I would soon discover that all of the temples had too many rare statues, historical points, founding stories, and sheer beauty of landscape and architecture to adequately absorb. Mostly, I had to let the spirit of each sacred site flow over and through me in much the same way Christians let the divine reading of scripture (or *lectio divina*), pour over and through them, letting God's truth be revealed. So too, Kannon's wisdom would arise spontaneously out of contemplation and reflection.

Already late afternoon, the temple would soon close. We had to find the office where they sold the *nokyocho*, or pilgrim's book, a place where the temple steward records the pilgrim's visit.

Reluctantly, we re-entered the "crowd stream" and let ourselves be carried along like two kayakers running the rapids. A little building right after the hondo held promise of our intended destination. We carefully maneuvered toward our access point, made ground, and stepped inside a shop selling books, incense and other pilgrim paraphernalia. The clerk, all aflutter now at the two *gaijin* (foreigners) expressing interest in the Kannon pilgrimage, showed us a rainbow-colored brocade book with thirty-three pastel temple images and thirty-three blank pages for the seal and calligraphy. We crooned delight, and purchased two with a box of incense; then proceeded next door to the *nokyo* to receive our first Kannon pilgrimage "we were here" stamp.

The smiling priest, equally impressed with these two Western "ladies" on their way to the remote hinterlands of the Kii Peninsula, stamped our book as we watched him perform the ritual of *Shodo*, the Way of the Brush, overlaying the temple seal with the name of the temple and the date of our visit. Calligraphy looked deceptively easy, yet like all of the "Dos" or "Ways" of Japan, it took years and years of practice and discipline to be able to perform "brush writing" with ease and grace; and like all of the Dos, Shodo involved the spiritual practice of observing the mind and letting thoughts go by like so much flotsam in a mountain stream. Perhaps for the priest, the years of "stamping" thousands of pilgrim's books had smoothed away any boredom or irritation that might plague a person in his job.

When finished, the priest handed us our books with a satisfied smile. We handed him the customary 300 yen donation, but he declined to take it. Instead he sent us on our way with encouraging words, a packet of white paper slips, and instructions on what to do with the paper slips—"prayer" slips we discovered later.

With the thousands of pilgrims and tourists who pass through the nokyo every day, the priest's cheerful and generous disposition, so remarkable under the circumstances, made a lasting impression on us, and served to remind how small seemingly insignificant acts of kindness can impact an individual, a city, a country and the world. Ah, our first live bodhisattva experience!

With the priest's blessings and incense in hand we returned to the censer to offer the symbolic three sticks for the three jewels, but the large bronze cauldron heaped with the ash of thousands of incense sticks, had been covered and shut down for the day. Disappointed that we hadn't been able to complete our pilgrim rituals, we nevertheless continued on our way toward the vermillion pagoda in the distance, now illuminated by the late afternoon sun; it beckoned with the promise of liberation, as it had for millennia, and never let us forget that Buddha consciousness existed in the here and now. "Do not seek elsewhere," he had advised 2,500 years ago.

Swept along by the devotional and not so devotional, we tried to hang on to that thread of meaning. The pagoda lured us forward with its mystical aura, so too the next purification station, the Otawa no Taki, a natural spring that has been pouring forth healing water since the days when Priest Enchin dreamed of finding the source of the Yodo River and built his hermitage where Kiyomizudera now stands "bringing coolness to everyone's soul."

Although not a required ritual, it seemed a shame to pass up the chance for even more purification and blessings by foregoing the long line of devotees. We took our place and "cupping our hands" sipped from the wish-granting stream. I prayed for the release of delusions, and true to my request, before we made our final departure from Kiyomizudera, we visited the Daizuigu-do, the symbolic birth canal of Daizuigu Bodhisattva — *Mahapratisara* in Sanskrit — a manifestation of Kannon, and the most memorable experience of our visit.

Once again we removed our shoes, but this time we carried them along with us in a plastic bag and descended a narrow staircase into a dark tunnel. Before we disappeared into total blackness, the temple attendant advised: "No attachment," and "Hang onto rosary." He meant the over-sized wooden rosary at the bottom of the stairs that served as a handrail. We were not to let go under any circumstances. But what did he mean about attachment?

I led the way into pitch darkness. The absence of light made it impossible to tell whether the last step had been reached, or if one more would catch my foot unaware and send me tumbling into oblivion. I moved rather tentatively. My sister, growing impatient with my pace, urged me to go faster. Not knowing what to expect, and with no idea how long we would remain in total darkness, or what would, could, should happen to us down there, I had to trust. And I certainly had to let go, of everything — no attachment. The experience felt like the process of dying and passing from this life to another, of being in what Tibetans call the *bardo* between death and re-birth.

Like the blind, I had no sight, only touch. The uneven wood of the rosary beads running under my palm and the stone floor polished smooth by thousands of pilgrim's feet compelled me onward into the darkness and uncertainty.

Before claustrophobia or sheer panic set in, a dim light appeared around a bend in the "birth canal," but it wasn't the end of the journey, only a reminder that this was not a Halloween experience but a sacred experience. A revolving Sanskrit letter carved into a large smooth stone and lit from above, came into view like a visionary dream; Daizuigu's Sanskrit "seed letter" represented the deity herself. We were to hold this image at our heart while making a request. I think I requested liberation, or something like that, recognizing that only ignorance and deluded thinking kept me from realizing my true self. Soon after a brighter light appeared and we were born back into daylight, but not our old lives; we had symbolically left them back in the previous world.

The journey into the bodhisattva's birth canal instilled lingering thoughts about my own impermanence and the final letting go: my precious human form. Fear of death, perhaps the underlying motivation for all spiritual pilgrimage, compelled me to search for the truth of life before death claimed me. I suspected that all I needed to know resided in the timeless present; and over the course of the pilgrimage, from conception onwards, I continually felt that "now" my pilgrimage had begun. In fact, it was always beginning in each new moment, some moments more dramatic, illuminating or poetic than others, but in essence always the forever now of life—sometimes quiet and peaceful, sometimes loud and busy, sometimes dull and mundane, and always—no matter how much we thought we were in control— uncertain. That remained the difficult part: the uncertainty of life, the impermanence of that which we loved and cherished. And yet this changing face of Beingness brought forth the excitement, mystery and delight of life, as long as one could remain open and accepting—not attached.

Daizuigo's birth canal lent a feeling of calm acceptance to the process of death. We simply left one world and soon emerged in another. I imagined my formless self as water in a ceramic container. If the container shattered into a hundred pieces the water would simply flow out unobstructed.

* * *

As the sun dropped into the distant mountains surrounding Kyoto, we came to the end of the circuitous path that led us to the exit of our first pilgrimage temple. My last memory of Kiyomizudera remains that of re-entering the "crowd stream" and letting ourselves be carried along through the rest of the

19

compound until we reached the narrow street of tea shops, ceramic stores, restaurants, and the never ending river of pilgrims going up and down the hill. The sun had nearly set and the shops in the labyrinth-like side streets were closing for the day. We too headed home—back to our efficiency inn— exhausted, exhilarated, questioning, and ultimately filled with the blessings and ponderings of the day's events.

Chapter 3

Although my heart
Is little concerned
With the next life,
Kannon's vow is as heavy
As this Stone Mountain

Ishiyamadera – Temple 13

Genji's Tale

Immortalized in woodblock prints by Hiroshige and Yoshitoshi, Ishiyamadera (Temple 13) will forever be remembered and loved as the retreat center where Lady Murasaki Shikibu penned the first novel known to the world: *The Tale of Genji*. Like the story itself—a Heian Period masterpiece of poetic subtleties—Ishiyamadera mesmerized with its folding screen of autumn maples painted across the vast hillside of Mt. Sekikozan. Reds, oranges and golds overlaid and intertwined with cryptomeria, pine and bamboo, with gray roof tiles and wooden verandahs, statues and the monolithic stones that give Ishiyamadera its solid ancient power—and its name (Stone Mountain Temple). Pilgrims donning colorful umbrellas moved up and down the steep stone staircases like animated flowers, alleviating the weighty feel of the thousands of lives, stories and dramas that have passed through this temple complex over the centuries. The ubiquitous sound of ravens cawing remained absent on this day, replaced instead by the sound of rain gushing through bamboo gutters. I imagined Lady Murasaki sitting on a verandah looking out toward Lake Biwa in the distance, her twelve-layers of perfectly coordinated Heian period pastel kimono flowing behind her as she created the character of Lord Genji, an impossibly handsome, unusually talented young prince who craved the company and conquest of women—both young and old. Visitors and pilgrims come to Ishiyamadera to get a taste of the author who is portrayed in a Noh drama *Genji Kuyo* as a manifestation of Kannon. Pilgrims also come to pray for the end of addictions—the notable healer being Nyoirin Kannon (Wish-fulfilling Kannon) only displayed every 33 years or whenever a new emperor is enthroned.

I never discovered the legendary reason why the Kannon at Ishiyamadera is known for healing addictions, and at first I didn't see how addictions related to Lady Murasaki and Lord Genji either. But sometimes the obvious is, well, not obvious. After my second read of *The Tale of Genji*, I saw how Lady Murasaki had created a character completely driven by his addictions—namely, sexual conquest. Genji preyed on every woman who caught his fancy, including a ten-year-old girl whom he abducted so that she could be molded into the quintessential femme fatale of his desire, all the while leaving a trail of female ruin and broken hearts across the poetic landscape of ancient Japan—not to mention a legacy of sexual aggression that can only be described as, well, rape; and all this by a man—and culture—who claimed to be Buddhist? Hmm!

With *The Tale of Genji* as the subtext to Ishiyamadera, I wondered what Buddha had to say about the repercussions of sexual addiction? What did Kannon, with her eyes of compassion, want us to know about such matters?

Under the precepts that guide the life of a Mahayana Buddhist, we have the advice: "refrain from sexual misconduct," or "do not misuse sexuality." The precept of "refraining from sexual misconduct" is not a commandment, but a guideline or wise recommendation meant to reduce or eliminate suffering and the negative karmic repercussions of one's actions. Sexual misconduct can arise in many forms, from flirting inappropriately, to using derogatory language, cheating on someone you promised monogamy, to sexually violent crimes and child pornography.

In the *Pali Canon*, the closest document we have to Buddha's actual teachings, Buddha gave a discourse on the "three kinds of unrighteous bodily conduct." Sexual misconduct is one of these three. Even though the advice he gives relates mostly to men and asks them to refrain from intercourse with any woman who is married, engaged, protected by a parent, relative or the law, we have to take these teachings within the cultural context of ancient India, and in general say that any sexual conduct—by a man or a woman—that harms oneself or another is "sexual misconduct."

In Lord Genji's time, a woman who became widowed would often become a nun—the only way she could respectfully remove herself from the predatory behavior of men, and the manipulation of fathers and mothers who, out of cultural conditioning, conspired to arrange a daughter's marriage prospects for business, societal or political reasons. Many women pursued artistic paths once relieved of the obligation (and sometimes burden) of the sexually involved relationship game.

Buddhism had, by the time of Lady Murasaki and Lord Genji, become a powerful religious force, but the admonition to refrain from sexual misconduct, or sexual greed as some would say, remained as difficult to follow back then as it is today. Buddhist temples in our modern world, supposed paragons of ethical behavior, have experienced sexual scandal: broken vows, violated precepts, unchecked predatory behavior between teachers and students that have left spiritual communities disenchanted, skeptical and, in some cases, devastated. We too had our Genjis.

By middle-age, Genji started to rethink his life. Toward the end of the novel he contemplates impermanence—as he and others periodically do throughout the book—and turns his attention toward preparing for his next incarnation. He doesn't reflect on his sexual misconduct—in that era his behavior was considered acceptable, possibly normal—only on the fleeting nature of existence.

At Ishiyamadera, I made prayers for the end of addictions, and reflected on the many addictions that permeate Western culture—all manifestations of our attachment to sensual pleasure and our aversion to being in the present moment, alone with our pain, discomfort, grief, sadness, yearning, anger, self-loathing, shame and all the other umpteen different faces of human suffering. Today we see lives ruined by adultery, pedophilia, rape and other forms of sexual violence. Even fashion, at least in the West, has programmed us with a desire to be sexy and alluring at any cost: monetary, comfort, safety (check out those five inch strappy stilettos). And didn't it seem that everyone these days revealed cleavage at one end or the other?

Without being moralistic, I wondered how young women (but also young men), were fairing with the constant bombardment of sexual advertising and sexual expectation foisted on them by the hungry machine of capitalism. In many ways, sexual exploitation in 21st-century American culture had only assumed new layers of subtle and not so subtle expectation. Since the 1960s, we were now said to have choices, freedom, sexual liberation.... But I saw a lot of evidence to the contrary. And only a year after the completion of my pilgrimage, the 2016 presidential elections would reveal a shocking layer of sexism lurking beneath the surface of American culture.

* * *

An artistic, poetic heart, reflected in Lord Genji's better moments, saves him from being an absolute scoundrel. And despite his sex addiction and predatory drive, we see a Genji who loves music, excels at poetry, has mastered subtleties, believes in integrity and honor and who looks after his offspring—more than we can say for many of our own society's scoundrels. Ultimately we forgive Prince Genji whose character mirrors all that we desire and all that lies dormant within us. Compassion is, after all, what Kannon imparts—compassion for ourselves and others even with all our unlimited and uniquely imperfect ways.

Chapter 4

The moon,
Glittering between the waves
As the rippling sound
From the bell at Miidera
Shines over the lake

Miidera – Temple 14

Mara's Conquest

A day of relentless rain and rubbery legs from stair climbing brought us to the base of Miidera, Temple 14, where leaky shoes and soggy socks left little enthusiasm for this "pilgrimage." On the other hand, getting too cozy and comfortable in our little human form (or too attached to the lure of comfort) contradicted Buddhist teachings about happiness residing inside, not outside in external conditions. Better to relinquish any clinging to pleasurable preferences and get on with it.

Even so, Miidera presented other challenges: another round of stair climbing—steep stone stairs made slippery from the relentless rain—and nothing very inspiring to commend it except, per our guidebook, a remarkable wood carving of a dragon and a famous bell said to have "the most beautiful sound of any bell in Japan." The dragon remains in my memory. But ringing the bell? Neither of us remembers a bell.

Miidera, once one of the four largest temple complexes in Japan, didn't offer many spiritually inspiring moments that lingered after our visit—and I'd be lying if I said that every temple along the pilgrimage route produced unforgettable experiences. Perhaps the relentless rain "dampened" our enthusiasm, but Miidera, even now, remains a blur of stone stairs leading up to the lower temple, the level where, in days past, the women were allowed to visit. Once again the men—the ones in power—saved the lofty heights for themselves. But like all things "lofty," the temple had fallen from power into an ordinary neighborhood temple with a few historical artifacts.

Due to Miidera's modern day ordinariness, coupled with its history of decline, it elicited more insight than temples known for their beauty and sacred emanations. Miidera taught how to accept the now in whatever form it arises, not to expect bedazzlement by the next greatest event or object. In this way, the pilgrimage, as in life, revealed a pattern of ordinary and extraordinary, of steep and confronting mountain slopes with gradual and even flat entry points. The entire route became a metaphor for the highs and lows of life, the easy and the challenging, the forgettable and the unforgettable, the sacred and the profane. One of the values of pilgrimage lay in acknowledging and accepting this pattern. To look back at the stairs already climbed can be interesting but of no great importance, and to look ahead to the steep climb ahead only puts fear and anxiety into one's heart. Better to go along and enjoy the unique beauty of each step, each tuft of moss, each red maple or golden ginkgo leaf, each drop of rain making its way into one's shoes.

Miidera, a teaching on how time changed circumstances, pointed to all things that pass: empires, kingdoms, presidents, and vast temple communities (or countries) once wielding power and privilege. Everyone and everything falls from material grace eventually. Power over others, usually fueled by greed and attachment, cannot be sustained. Inevitably nature finds a way to bring those at the top of the mountain down to the valley.

Perceptions too, come and go. They are not static, but empty of anything fixed. There is no inherently existing Miidera— nothing frozen in time and place. On another day, at another time, under different circumstances, Miidera would appear as something else. After all, sacredjapan.com described Miidera's main temple hall as "one of the most beautiful buildings in

Japan."

On a cold and rainy day in autumn Miidera showed up in my field of vision and presented itself as a teaching on power. A photo I took, a tall white Mother Kannon, with a blue flag flapping in the wind, stands out among the dark brown wood, gray roof tiles and long gray stone staircases that make up Miidera and my memory. A feeling of something lost lingered in the air: the skeletal remains of a long ago life. But Kannon presided over all and warmed us with her motherly, protective gaze. She represented the life that still lingered here, and the reason to visit. The great impermanent wave of human history washed over this temple compound and whispered, "let go of attachment," to power, privilege, wealth, influence, prestige. It will all disappear in due course anyway and no one will remember or care that you were once "great."

Mara, that wily demon depicted in many guises in the Buddhist story, attempted to distract Siddhartha, the future Buddha, from his quest for enlightenment by tempting him with worldly power (among other things). Mara, a metaphor for all that deters us from the spiritual path, makes worldly life look attractive and alluring. In the 11th century, clashes between Miidera and Enryakuji over religious doctrine and political leadership, erupted into warfare. Miidera, eventually burned to the ground by the warrior monks of Mt. Hiei who outnumbered the warrior monks of Miidera, succumbed to the perils of power. Both historically and currently, those motivated by greed and hatred, create the greatest folly. They too will perish and leave ruins in the great turning of cyclic existence.

Chapter 5

On Kannon's island paradise,
Waves crash upon the shores;
In the sacred land of Kumano,
Down Nachi Mountain,
The thundering waterfall cascades

Seigantoji – Temple 1

Eternal Stream of Compassion

Marvels and mysteries of ancient and modern Japan unfolded from our train window as we headed down the Kii Peninsula toward Seigantoji: Temple 1 of the Saigoku Pilgrimage. White wind turbines scattered across undulating mountain tops twirled into blue sky like wings of prehistoric birds; tangerine groves on perfectly terraced hillsides hung heavy with lollipop fruit plump and ready for the picker's hand; along the coast, monolithic rock formations sticking straight up in their massiveness looked as if dropped by some benevolent god intent on preventing the next tsunami. The mammoth boulders stood like stop signs to the power of nature.

As we neared "the sacred land of Kumano" the giant stones told of a "cosmic bridge" created by Kobo Daishi, the 9th-century Shingon bodhisattva residing in meditative equipoise on the top of Mt. Koya. Some said the stones were the bridge to Kannon's Pure Land thought to be somewhere in the southern sea.

Whether a bridge, a stop sign or some other cosmic indicator, neither god nor bodhisattva nor mammoth stones had been able to hold back the giant wave that rolled in from the sea on March 11th, 2011 crushing, smashing or drowning everything in its wake. On a Friday afternoon in winter, while children were still at school, life for millions of coastal dwellers along Japan's

Pacific coast changed forever. The 9.0 earthquake shifted the earth's axis, caused icebergs to collapse in Antarctica and set off a nuclear meltdown at the Fukushima Daiichi Power Plant.

Traveling so close to this temperamental sea took my thoughts into the ghostly realm that haunted all: the unpredictable and precarious nature of our precious human lives. At least momentarily my trance of false-security was shaken. It had been less than 18 months since the worst tsunami in recorded Japanese history struck the far northern coast from where we were. I remembered the stories broadcast on television, radio and internet; the film footage of "the wave" playing again and again as it washed over everything in its path, including trains, like ours. The Great East Japan Earthquake, and the Wave that transcended and collapsed 39-foot seawalls, eliminated over 18,000 school children, babies, grandparents, housewives, laborers, fishermen, and even the young woman on the third floor of the Crisis Management Department who stayed at her post warning others to flee to higher ground. She too was swept away, microphone in hand, still warning others to run.

I counseled myself to be ready to leave this life at any second, to be ready to give up all that I cherished. I wondered in a moment of reverie in what ways my existence mattered, in what ways my non-existence would matter. Would my leaving be any more significant than a ripe tangerine falling to the ground? My life: the play of form and emptiness on the cosmic movie screen of existence had an ending that nobody knew.

Catastrophes make us pause and take stock of our lives — or at least they should. It was hard to remove the blinders and admit that something like a tidal wave could happen to me as easily as it happened to "them." And yet I found myself ruminating over what I would do, think, or feel if a wall of seawater suddenly came hurtling toward our train.

As we continued along the coast, images of modern-day Japan, imaginary tsunamis, flashbacks of my life, interwove into a dreamlike landscape of thought, perception and sensation. The view out the window, like my mind-stream, and my life, kept changing. We left the coast, and headed into mountains (or perhaps the other way around). Thoughts of tidal waves gave way to the reality of electric power lines strung across every hill top. The beauty of nature had been lost in trade for dishwashers, microwaves, computers, TVs, air-conditioning, and all the rest of our electronic gadgets. Mountain summits, once places of sacred refuge, now resembled the arms of junkies riddled with needle tracks.

Not long after the unsightly maze of the Japanese power grid, our train pulled into Kii-Katsuura, our final stop. All ruminations aside, we frantically collected our bags and exited into a small town train station. Outside, as if on cue, the right bus pulled up at the right time and off we went toward the distant mountains. En route the primeval forest of Kumano Kodo, containing another series of sacred pilgrimage trails beckoned with possibilities for future hiking. But for now, our destination was Temple 1, and a small hamlet at the base of Nachi Falls where we would spend the night.

After we found our inn and dropped our bags, we asked a woman on the street the way to Seigantoji. She smiled and pointed to a flight of steep stone stairs that switch-backed up the hill. Ah, the ubiquitous "steep stone stairs," the great metaphor for life: a difficult path shrouded in mystery that required a great amount of effort and fortitude. After four hours sitting on a train and another forty minutes on a bus, initially it felt good to be walking again. But this pleasure, like many others, manifested as the suffering of change—nothing pleasurable could be sustained very long without it becoming uncomfortable. As I huffed and puffed my way to the first landing, and silently cursed the daunting sight of endless steps without end, I temporarily lost sight of my reasons for doing this *pilgrimage*. The trek to the temple top involved more stairs than the previous one, and each one tested my resolve to do the pilgrimage no matter how strenuous the conditions (although we had yet to discover that the "steep stone stairs" of Seigantoji were a cake walk compared to the upcoming hikes to Sefukuji and Kami Daigoji).

Once we made it to the top, and began our ablutions and rituals, the long climb up receded into the background of memory. Happiness returned, along with a renewed sense of excitement and purpose about what lay ahead. Yet, already late afternoon, the temple would close soon. No time to dally. We got our pilgrim's stamp, made prayers, bought a box of incense and continued along to the Hall of Lanterns and the Sanjudo Pagoda. We climbed to the top of the pagoda to view the valley below and Nachi Falls in the distance. The Falls—as depicted in countless postcards and travel brochures, and considered to be the highest waterfall in Japan—cascaded over a high precipice and roared to the river below; the waterfall was the main attraction and reason Seigantoji came into existence.

Captivated and awed by the mystery of Nachi Falls, we wondered where all that water came from. No nearby snow-capped mountains or melting glaciers explained the abundance of water flowing continuously over the high cliff, yet one ton of water drops from the falls every second. Said to be a metaphor for Kannon's continuous and unending compassion, perhaps my wonderment lay somewhere in imagining, or knowing, that this power of compassion could be found as the nature of our own essence—if only we could pierce through the gauzy dreamlike cloud of false perceptions said to obscure our Buddhanature, and open our hearts wide without fear.

The powerful Nachi Falls—where Kannon first appeared to Priest Ragyō—led to the founding of Seigantoji; thus the government preserved the surrounding forests as a pilgrimage destination as this had been a sacred land for over a thousand years. Designated a UNESCO World Heritage Site, Kumano would be preserved in perpetuity much like we preserve wilderness areas in our National Park system. Nachi Falls could be our Yosemite Falls, a place of power that Native people and John Muir (and perhaps a handful of other folks) considered holy. But why didn't we think of Yosemite Falls as the unending flow of female compassion? Where were our sacred metaphors? Would we be more inclined to protect and preserve nature's bounty and diversity if we as a culture had formed a deeper kinship with our feminine nature? I had to believe that our willingness to degrade the environment had much to do with how we degraded women and the feminine.

Leaving the Pagoda, we walked downhill toward the sound of roaring water. At the entrance to the falls area, a wide granite staircase through old growth forest allowed dozens of pilgrims at a time to descend to the bottom. One could feel the magnetic attraction of surging water pulling one towards its magnificence. Before long I could feel the spray from Nachi Fall's 436-foot drop, like Kannon's blessings anointing my being. No amount of shutter snapping could do it justice—only watching, listening, absorbing, being. When a bus load of tourists arrived, we receded into the background and headed to our inn. Through thick forest and diminishing light of early evening, I glanced back occasionally to catch a glimpse of this magical "thundering waterfall," but there was no possessing something so grand and mysterious. As John Muir often said, nature alone out did all the temples and cathedrals made by humans. Did we need anything else?

Once a place of austere purification practices whereby priests stood beneath the icy waterfall waiting for spiritual revelation, Nachi Falls today could be seen as our own unlimited potential: endless and abundant. Much as Dogen Zenji, the founder of Soto Zen in the 13th century indicated when he proclaimed that we were already enlightened—meaning that wisdom and compassion made up the very ground of our being rather than qualities to be gained or achieved, or found anywhere else but inside. We only had to recognize it. With all the exotic spiritual practices coming out of the East, perhaps we had forgotten, or never considered, that enlightenment itself was not exotic, but our original nature waiting to be rediscovered.

* * *

The morning before our departure, we made one last trip to the base of Nachi Falls. The day promised to be cool but pleasantly sunny. Tour buses hadn't arrived yet. We had the great compassionate metaphor to ourselves. I walked down the grand granite staircase feeling like a princess at a ball. At the bottom, the hostess greeted me with a fine mist and a roar. I accepted her hospitality and silently extolled my gratitude. Her vaporous breath gently fell upon my face and hair and I eagerly accepted her blessings.

Chapter 6

The place of my birth
Is far away from here,
Kimiidera,
Capital of the cherry blossoms,
Feels closer than home

Kimiidera – Temple 2

Gifts from the Dragon King

Izumi Shikibu, one of the *Thirty-Six Medieval Poetry Immortals* of the Heian Period, once had a dream in which she realized that Kannon moves among us in disguise. I interpreted this in two ways: disguised within ourselves to ourselves and disguised as ordinary others. For the next couple of days, we were about to experience Kannon disguised as "ordinary others."

Earlier in the month, I had e-mailed the Kyoto Service of Goodwill Guides (SGG Club) to inquire about assistance traveling to Seigantoji in Wakayama prefecture; that e-mail, forwarded to the coordinator of an English language volunteer guide in Wakayama City, got forwarded to a fellow Club member. A long series of e-mails ensued whereby the last recipient of the e-mail chain, a Mr. Hiro Kitagami, offered to pick us up at the Wakayama City train station and *drive* us to Temple 2, 3 and 4. Wow! Really? He also suggested that we stay overnight at Mr. Ito's, an artist friend in Kinokawa City who ran a kind of International House for foreigners. Since Ito-san's house, a mere ten-minute walk to Temple 3, sounded like the easiest option for our second overnight, we took the path of least resistance. Yet, not having met either gentleman left us a bit hesitant. We briefly, very briefly, entertained fantasies of unsavory types cruising for unsuspecting tourists through the internet. If this had been any other country, we might have paid heed to our fears, but in Japan we hardly gave them a second thought. I dismissed any hesitation as cautionary habit. More likely, we would be met by a kind, generous and hospitable guide eager to practice his English and help us understand and appreciate Japanese culture. It was highly unlikely that Mr. Kitagami ran a gang of rogue gaijin snatchers who would rob us of money and passport and leave us stranded in the primeval forest of the Kii Peninsula.

Even so, a tiny fragment of doubt lingered—at least up until the moment we entered the Wakayama train station and beheld our first "gang" member: an attractive *woman*, smartly dressed in gray kimono and colorful obi holding a sign that said, "Welcome Gwen and Joan Stamm."

We laughed later at our previous venture into anything resembling trepidation. Instead we surrendered to the presence of Kannon now manifesting as Junko Nakaura*: calligrapher, piano teacher, mother, and English club friend of Hiro Kitagami.

Junko-san escorted us outside where our e-mail guy—self-described as an old man with glasses wearing a khaki baseball cap—waited to meet us. Hiro-san stood next to his car, parked in a load-unload zone. Yes, he had glasses and wore a baseball cap, but old? Well, not much older than us, he was also rugged, fit, energetic and happy to be of assistance.

After much bowing, handshaking, and words of appreciation, we—and perhaps they too—breathed a sigh of relief that everyone appeared to be relatively normal and harmless. With good cheers all around, we got into Hiro's compact car and headed off to Kimiidera, also known as Kongohoji (Temple of the Vajra Jewel). Once we arrived at the temple grounds and Hiro parked the car, he opened his cooler and offered us cookies and oranges; then he brought out two thermos bottles and offered us tea and coffee. We accepted cookies and tea; they drank coffee; and together we tried to have a conversation about our reasons for embarking on a Kannon pilgrimage.

I attempted to explain in simple English what wasn't so simple: my attraction to the *female* Buddha of Compassion—a spiritual icon that we lacked in modern Western culture except for some mystical versions of Mary; my background in Catholicism, which no doubt had planted seeds of devotional practices; and the power of visiting sacred sites that held imprints left by thousands over millennia. But truth be told, all my reasons were not completely apparent even to myself. I could tell by the look on Hiro's and Junko's faces that my feeble explanation wasn't quite translating. They listened kindly, with appropriate nods and polite gestures of understanding, but whether they had any feeling for "pilgrimage" other than facilitating ours and others' (Hiro had helped his mother complete the pilgrimage years back), remained a mystery.

After our snack, we set out for the top of Kimiidera, up the— you guessed it—steep stone stairs (231 to be exact). I read that in early spring the steps to this temple complex are awash in cherry blossoms, from trees that, according to Buddhist lore, came from one of the Dragon Kings who lives in the sea. I didn't understand completely at the time why dragons figured so prominently in Buddhist mythology, or why they were one of the eight mythological creatures that guarded Buddhism, but they appeared everywhere: as purification fonts, decorative motifs, and even large bronze statues intertwined with Kannon.

In the Lotus Sutra, a teaching highly revered throughout Japan, the Dragon King's daughter—an eight-year-old no less (eight being an overall auspicious number)—is the only female in all of Buddhist teachings who attained enlightenment (much to the dismay of Shariputra, Buddha's leading disciple, who didn't believe any female could attain enlightenment let alone a mere girl). The Dragon King's daughter basically told the assembly of disciples, hey, you don't have to practice for a gazillion lifetimes, you can become an awakened being now. And in the amount of time it took to present Buddha with a precious gift, she attained enlightenment.

Shariputra's initial skepticism over female enlightenment indicated to me that no matter how awake someone is purported to be, our perception of the world—in any era on the time continuum—is limited and culturally conditioned, and that making assumptions about what is real or attainable or possible based on what we cognize with ordinary human (and therefore imperfect) vision is open to error. This ancient and popular Sutra speaks of realities beyond those norms accepted at the time, and perhaps of realities that even today we may not grasp—stories of mythological creatures (non-humans) who have wisdom and advanced knowledge.

The founding legend of Kimiidera involved the priest and founder Ikō, who spent several years in the nearby sea imparting teachings to the Dragon King. What could Priest Ikō have taught the Dragon King other than how to harness his own power for the good of all? Kannon and the dragon intertwined; the peaceful and the wrathful, the male and the female, wisdom and compassion—not to be feared but used to overcome that part of us that wants to remain small, fearful, timid—unenlightened.

In turn, the Dragon King, upon his teacher's departure, gave him three gifts: a temple bell, a conch-shell trumpet and seven cherry tree seeds. The cherry trees at Kimiidera are said to have descended from the Dragon King's gift.

Naturally the fantastical legends surrounding Kimiidera imbued the place with a special essence, even though cherry trees wouldn't bud for another four months. I took it all in, absorbed what I could, and marveled at the statue of six-armed Nyoirin Kannon (Omnipotent Kannon) with her head tilted to one side toward the hand that represents her vow to save all beings from the hell realms. Her other five hands represent her vow to save all beings from the human, god, demi-god, animal and hungry ghost realms. Old and artistically carved out of stone, the artist had captured Kannon's wise and loving nature. I took several photos, only to be disappointed later when an electric cord ran through the background of every shot but one.

Kimiidera, steeped in dragon lore, Kannon appearances, and visionary dreams held a feeling of blessedness within its ancient walls—something special had happened here, could still happen here. The Three Sacred Wells of Purity, Healing and Good Fortune; the golden Kannon implanted into the womb of a Living Kannon; the "vajra jewel" a double-pronged ritual implement that symbolizes Indestructible Truth or the wisdom of "emptiness"; and the legend involving the Dragon King residing in the waters of Wakanoura Bay (Bay of Poetry) all pointed to the one truth of the Awakened Mind or Pure Presence—the essence of Kannon permeated all.

Unpacking the layers of symbol and metaphor prompted a conversation with a friend who suggested drawing a map with Kimiidera at the center. What I saw after completing my rudimentary drawing were four stick figures ascending a staircase into the realm of a living Kannon: our own true nature. I saw two of us as guides and two being guided, but all of us being brought together by the power of the Kannon pilgrimage. Something greater than our individual selves, yet not separate from ourselves, directed our course. Golden Kannon in the womb of Living Kannon, symbolized the two and the one shining brightly on this sunny day in autumn, a November day in Japan—two Japanese, two Americans, all of us with individual bodies, but sharing an essence. Together we admired the view of city and waterfront, the same city that American B-29 Superfortress bombers firebombed in 1945 destroying half of the city and killing thousands of civilians. One could easily see why Kannon, the great metaphor of compassion would often be depicted with 1,000 arms reaching out to those in every quarter of the universe suffering under the weight and sheer agony of human ignorance.

At Kimiidera both eleven-headed and thousand-armed Kannons are held as "secret" icons, only to be publicly revealed every 50 years. The Kannon erected for public viewing, a 36-foot high thousand-armed Kannon completely covered in gold leaf, towered above onlookers like a beacon of bright sunlight. As we entered the new mausoleum to view what I would later regard as "Sun Goddess" Kannon, Hiro and Junko waited patiently while we took in the mammoth icon that they had probably seen dozens of times. To them, the more interesting aspect of the mausoleum was on the second floor, above the Kannon statue, where a wide veranda encircling the entire building offered the best view of city and sea. But for me, even though I didn't care for the artistry of this glitzy Kannon, it conjured images of the Sun Goddess Amaterasu, and the original goddess culture of ancient days. One could easily see that worship of Amaterasu had been absorbed into Buddhism as worship of Kannon, not an unusual evolution when it comes to new religions establishing themselves into indigenous cultures with existing religious practices. It indicated that the manifestation of Wisdom and Compassion had simply changed form according to the times.

By mid-afternoon, many of the "points of interest" at Kimiidera blurred into a collage of images, impressions, snippets of conversation and inspirations to be filed away and carefully examined later. In this regard, I don't remember if we saw all three of the famous sacred wells or not. But even so, in our own metaphorical dream journey, I liked to think that the Well of Good Fortune produced Hiro and Junko, and perhaps the Well of Healing erased some small vestiges of the past still lingering in the minds that remembered that our ancestors had once been "enemies." I hoped that the Well of Purity cleansed us from fear and negativity and let us see the true dynamic that all humans shared: that we all wanted to be happy and live without suffering.

The four of us, at least for a few hours, traveled together in the holy realm of Kannon's Kimiidera, surrounded by a myriad of symbols pointing to the Indestructible Truth of our own existence. Temple of the Vajra Jewel, like a diamond: bright and rare; like a thunderbolt of power, the energy we needed to propel us into our own unfathomable consciousness.

Hiro and Junko: two ordinary Japanese citizens? Or two extraordinary bodhisattvas? Either way, they facilitated our pilgrimage to Kimiidera and helped us fulfill our pilgrim's vow. Before heading off to Kinokawa City, Hiro dropped Junko at her house for an afternoon piano lesson; then the three of us took off to Temple 3: Kokawadera, another hour-long drive up the peninsula, and another venture into a new world.

* * *

Sadly, Junko Nakaura passed away in January, 2017 at the age of 54. She is survived by her husband and two daughters.

Chapter 7

My father and mother's
Kindness runs deeply
Kokawadera
Upon Kannon's vow
I can depend

Kokawadera – Temple 3

The Enchantment of Eight

By late afternoon we reached Kinokawa City, home of Kokawadera. The town looked like any other in Japan, a mixture of modern post-war construction with a few old-fashioned wood store fronts, gray temple roof tiles, and an occasional orange torii gate.

Hiro turned down a narrow residential street and slowed when he saw a small skinny guy wearing a black fleece vest and blue-jeans. Ito-san, with long gray pony tail carelessly tied back, waved us through his gate. A dog started barking—Ito's dog—and soon we were all out of the car bowing, shaking hands, exchanging greetings and trying to quiet the dog. But the usual time constraints hurried us through our greetings. Everyone knew that Temple 3 closed soon, and late afternoon was already upon us. We dropped our bags in the entry way of Ito-san's modern two-storey house and took off.

We had been told that Mr. Ito was about 80 years old, but the quickness and agility of his movements belied his age. We, at least 20 years younger, had to move quickly to keep up with his pace.

All along the way to the temple, friends and neighbors greeted our new host with waves and ride offers, or imparted some bit of information that made him smile. Mr. Ito returned the waves and smiles and declined the rides, even though he had to teach a children's English class in less than an hour. In addition, he had promised to make us dinner. After dinner we were invited to chat with members of his adult English Club, also coming to his house for dinner. Ito-san's energy seemed boundless.

The walk to Kokawadera along a flat city street, by far the easiest of any on the pilgrimage route, soon met up with the Kinokawa River. We crossed the river on a vermillion foot bridge, and stopped in front of the Daimon Gate to admire the Deva Kings who guarded the temple and all that it stood for. We had arrived without trains, buses, trams, cable cars, boats, or taxis. We didn't have to hike a mountain, a hill or even a set of steep stone stairs. Ah, life's occasional ease! Once safely delivered into the realm of Kokawadera: Powder River Temple, Ito-san bid us farewell and left us in the capable hands of Hiro-san.

Besides the impressive and ancient gate built out of zelkova wood and the two amazing temple guardians carved out of Japanese Judas trees, the most notable feature at Kokawadera was the Teien Rock Garden laid out along the length of the temple compound. Meant to evoke the eight scenic views in Shiga Prefecture, the garden, inspired by China's eight scenic views of Xiaoxing in modern Hunan Province, exemplifies yet another aspect of the sacred number eight. Other than the symbol for infinity itself, the number eight repeats in so many different forms in Buddhism; it simply cannot be ignored. We have the Eightfold Path, the Eight Auspicious Symbols, the Eight Great Bodhisattvas, the Eight Mythological Creatures, the Eight Dragon Kings, and the 8th of December as Buddha's enlightenment day.

Teien Garden, created in the 16th century and now listed as a Nationally Important Cultural Property, literally represented eight scenic views, but on another level one could surmise that they symbolized the eight cardinal directions of the entire universe. Nothing would be left out of the sphere of awakened existence, or Ultimate Truth. The eight scenes are represented with large boulders and cycads, a tropical looking palm that is not a palm but a seed plant grown in Okinawa—Japan's most southern island. These cycads are thought to be over 400 years old, which is actually young for a cycad. They can live up to 1,000 years. The cycad's longevity, an appropriate choice for a Buddhist temple garden, complimented the solid eternal feeling of the rocks and the Buddhist teachings that had already been in existence for over 2,500 years.

Due to the lateness of the day, we soon began our pilgrimage rituals at the temizuya, this time not the typical dragon, but an exquisite lotus blossom (the lotus being one of the Eight Auspicious Symbols that signify leaving the muddy waters of ignorance for the sunlight of enlightenment). The lotus font also honored and reminded the pilgrim of one of the legends surrounding this ancient temple. Like all Buddhist legends, it contained a deeper dharma teaching.

The story goes that a young girl from a nearby wealthy family had an incurable illness. Her parents had tried everything, but to no avail. Then one day a monk appeared and told each parent on separate occasions that Kannon had medicine that would cure their daughter; they only needed to visit Kokawadera and the rest would be revealed. With renewed faith in Kannon, the couple stood before an image of the Goddess of Mercy and prayed. In an instant, a lotus bud appeared; it magically opened and dropped a special medicinal seed into the mother's hand. Without hesitation, she quickly gave it to her daughter. Miraculously the young child was cured of her incurable illness.

Yes, the "seed" of enlightenment, of awakening to our true self, to our essence and rightful place in this divine play, surely greater than all material wealth. To realize and live from the understanding of Ultimate Truth would be the cure for us all. It was a simple lesson, but an important one, especially in modern times rife with global conflict, terror attacks, mass shootings, hate crimes, fear of immigrants, fear of "the other side," fear of just about everything. We needed now more than ever to open our hearts to differences and diversity. Compassion was really our only hope if we as a species, a planet, a global community wanted to survive and thrive.

* * *

We made our sublime ablutions in the symbolic realm of Buddha's enlightenment and ventured off to the cavernous hondo (the largest of any along the pilgrimage route). While I lit a candle and made prayers for the well-being of my deceased parents (as I did at every temple), Hiro chatted with the head monk, and Gwen wafted incense over her head in an act of further purification.

All day the weather had been sunny and mild, and although I had noticed some dark clouds gathering, once inside the hondo, and with the various distractions of rituals, book stamping, and a stunning gold relief carving of Kannon emanating light rays into a wave motif, I hadn't noticed that nature had shifted. The wind picked up and blew fall leaves across the temple pathways. A gust swirled into and through the main hall like dragon's breath. By the time we had finished our prayers and rituals, clouds had moved over Kokawadera. In the time it takes to bow before the Buddha, torrents of rain, along with thunder and lightening, broke free from the sky.

Confident that the day would remain sunny, we had left our umbrellas back at Ito's house. But not to worry. The head priest—as well as everyone else in this town it seemed—was a good friend of Ito-san. Three umbrellas instantly appeared. We ran out into the thunderstorm with heads shielded, but not much else. The thunder and lightening continued, and in my mind, our gifted umbrellas—although greatly appreciated— now became mini lightening rods.

What had been a perfectly peaceful and delightful day, had suddenly and inexplicably transformed into a potentially dangerous, life threatening situation. (On average, 24,000 people worldwide die from lightning strikes every year; and 240,000 are injured.) Impermanence, always lurking around every corner descended to remind me once again of the fragility and foolishness of clinging to anything, least of all a pleasant sunny day, or my own life. The tides could turn at the flick of an Up-Down umbrella button. One had to be continually prepared for the best or the worst, and to be aware that in every moment it was prudent to leave positive imprints, good feelings, love and radiant light rather than any lingering darkness, negative feelings, bad vibes, or worse.

When it rains in Japan, well, it pours. Impossible to dodge the many puddles on streets and sidewalks, I felt the water oozing into those leaky shoes once again. Our cotton pants looked as if plucked from the spin cycle. We walked as fast as our legs would move in order to minimize exposure, but by the time we turned onto Mr. Ito's street and landed on his doorstep, we were beyond soaked.

Hiro went off to the kitchen, and we ducked upstairs to our bedrooms. Since we had left most of our luggage in Kyoto, we didn't have a change of clothes. Luckily, black silk long johns that kind of looked like leggings and a black print night shirt that kind of looked like a short little dress had to pass for current fashion. (Gwen donned a similar get up.) Chilled but dry, we put on our new attire and went off to mingle.

As we descended the stairs into the lower level hallway, we smelled the aroma of burning logs. While *we* had been figuring out our dinner "costume," *Hiro* had been making a fire in the wood stove. We pulled our chairs in close to the roaring blaze and felt the intense heat permeate our chilled bodies. Steam rose from our socks like yesterday's thought forms. Before long, members of the English Club began to arrive. Nobody seemed to notice our odd dress, or perhaps they were too polite to make mention of it.

Ito-san returned home from teaching the kids and started stir frying yakisoba on a large griddle. When Gwen innocently mentioned that she liked *okonomiyaki* (a kind of Japanese savory pancake—literally "whatever you like grilled"), Ito-san got on the phone. Within minutes the local grocer and expert okonomiyaki maker arrived. He whipped up a batch in Ito's kitchen and poured a glob onto the grill. With beer, sake and okonomiyaki being passed around, we had inadvertently landed into a typical Japanese home party—a party of eight no less.

Although originally we'd had misgivings about being the English-speaking "entertainment" at Ito-san's weekly gathering (haunted by memories of our teaching days in Kobe), the English Club get-together turned out to be one of the highlights of our three-day trip to the Kii Peninsula. Amidst the gaiety and light-hearted discussion we somehow got on the subject of Hiroshima and Nagasaki, a topic that, to my utter amazement, never seemed to provoke anger or blame in the Japanese. I didn't know if that was out of politeness—since we were their guests— or if, as sometimes was expressed, the Japanese felt responsible. I thought of the belief in karma that ran through any Buddhist influenced culture like an underground river. Maybe it played a part, or maybe not: I didn't want to speculate. Years after WWII, General LeMay, who planned and implemented the firebombing campaign against 67 Japanese cities, would admit to General McNamara that if our side had lost the war, the U.S. would have been tried for war crimes—implying that the level of consciously targeted and executed destruction against the Japanese people had been unethical even under terms of war.

In the Pali Cannon, Buddha instructs his disciples in five gifts. And what is the first gift? Buddha clearly states, without any hesitation, that a noble disciple "gives up the destruction of life and abstains from it." Then he asks his disciples to reflect on the life of one who is worthy and says "abandon the destruction of life, abstain from the destruction of life; with the rod and weapon laid aside, they [worthy ones] are conscientious and merciful and dwell compassionately toward all living beings."

Kokawadera, founded on the principle that killing violated an unspoken code of ethical conduct, tells the story of a hunter named Otomo Kujiko who saw a bright light coming from a distant mountain. When he traveled to that location he came upon a dead deer. He saw it as a sign that killing was wrong, and so he repented for having taken the lives of so many innocent animals. He built a hermitage on that special place: Kazarakisan Mountain; then purified himself to atone for taking life. One day a mysterious child appeared with a message. The child told Otomo that he wanted to carve an image of Thousand-armed Kannon but would need seven days of solitude in order to finish. Otomo agreed to leave the child alone for seven days. When he returned to his hut the ascetic found a beautiful image of Kannon. The child had vanished, which led many to believe that the carver, an emanation of Kannon, became the carved.

The Buddha told his disciples, "By abstaining from the destruction of life, the noble disciple gives to immeasurable beings freedom from fear, hostility, and oppression, he himself will enjoy immeasurable freedom from fear, hostility, and oppression. This is the first of those great gifts and the fourth stream of merit."

Japan's constitution outlaws war as a means to settle international disputes. Whether such a clause was suggested by the Japanese Prime Minister Kijuro Shidehara or The Supreme Commander of the Allied Powers, Japan has enjoyed the gift of peace and freedom from hostile forces for nearly 70 years.

* * *

By the end of the party our clothes and socks had dried, which allowed us to sink back into that warm feeling of comfort, security and safety—unreliable friends that they are. The next morning we returned to Kokawadera to give back the umbrellas and spend more time viewing the impressive Teien Garden. While we wandered about, a monk offered us two dragon *ema*: small wooden plaques with the animal totem for that particular year of the zodiac. (Ito-san had telephoned ahead.) In Shinto—the native Japanese religion now mixed with Japanese Buddhism—the wish or prayer written on the back of the ema acts as a petition to the Shinto deities (or Buddhas and bodhisattvas) to grant a favor.

My wish was simple: May Hiro-san and Ito-san be blessed with good fortune.

* * *

Before we left Kinokawa, Ito-san showed us his artist studio out back where he created beautiful sumi paintings on translucent paper. Galloping horses, in a style he'd learned from a master teacher in Shanghai, dominated the collection. When I asked him why he painted so many horses he smiled and simply said, "I like horses."

With parting gifts and endless good wishes we bid Ito-san farewell and headed off with Hiro to our next destination, Sefukuji, also known as Makinodera: Temple at the End of the Sutra. Temple 4 is known for Bato Kannon, or Horse-headed Kannon, the protector of animals (especially horses).

Chapter 8

Deep mountain passes
Through cypress and pine forests
If you can make it
To Makinoodera
Like the pony
Your spirits will be lifted

Sefukuji (Makinoodera) – Temple 4

The Mountain of Sacred Wandering

After the downpour in Kinokawa and weather reports that indicated a possible repeat the following day, we tried to release Hiro from any feelings of obligation about taking us to Seifukuji. We argued that the drive would be a couple hours each way, and in the rain, well, it was just asking too much.

Hiro listened but had no intention of backing out.

Later that night we again argued that since the weather seemed too unpredictable and the drive too far, we would go back to Kyoto on the train and try Sefukuji another time.

But Hiro probably knew that public transport to Temple 4's remote location presented a daunting challenge; we would have to return on another long train ride to reach the vicinity and rely on a limited bus schedule. We would be two women alone in the mountains and might need a guide. We were going, he insisted, and that was that.

* * *

An hour into our journey, cityscapes and modern development gave way to mountainous terrain with narrow roads and a few hamlets built along the edges of mountain streams. Rarely had I seen a landscape in Japan so devoid of human habitation.

Over the long trip, Hiro played self-made recordings of old songs: Perry Como, Paul Anka, Frank Sinatra and an assortment of others. I could tell from his selection that he liked romantic ballads and singers with deep melodic voices. We discussed music and singers—our favorites, his favorites. As we chatted about music we approached the foot of Mt. Makinosan. The weather had cooperated so far—only a few spits of rain now and then. Hiro pulled into a mostly deserted parking lot. "Amazing Grace," sung by a woman who sounded like a professional singer we knew from our island home, came pouring out of his CD player. Although the voice wasn't hers, it had brought forth a feeling of home and conjured an image of all of our island friends showing up to be with us on pilgrimage.

Still overcast but not raining, we put on our backpacks and started out. Only a handful of other hikers and pilgrims had braved the rather cool fall day.

Near the beginning of the ascent, a gateway thick with hanging straw sandals announced that we were now entering a sacred place. Previous pilgrims had hung symbolic straw sandals as an offering to the guardian deity and dedicated the merit of their climb to all sentient beings. At this point it became very clear that the way up would be in direct contrast to the ease in which we arrived at Temple 3. The pilgrimage route had been designed in an irregular but repeating pattern of easy, more difficult, very difficult, most difficult. Sefukuji fell between very difficult and most difficult. Our guidebook described the path as "staggeringly steep in places, with steps bare inches wide."

Indeed, the trail to the top consisted of a continuous "steep stone staircase" built into the side of the mountain centuries ago; the steps switch-backed up Mt. Makinosan, past springs, shrines, a little hut said to contain the hair of Kobo Daishi (founder of Shingon Buddhism) and a statue of the Daishi, who had wandered through these mountains in search of spiritual truth as we were now, and as thousands of others had over centuries. This was the place where En no Gyoja—founder of Shugendo, a religious sect that incorporated Shinto, Taoism, esoteric Buddhism and Shamanism into its practices—spent time searching for his own connection to Ultimate Truth. This was the place where Maitreya, singled out in the Lotus Sutra as the future Buddha, held a special place of honor even above Kannon. And would the Future Buddha be a person, or many persons, as some believe—a collection of awakened beings coming into their highest state of realization in our own times? According to Buddha's discourses in the Lotus Sutra, there are already "innumerable and immeasurable" Buddhas existing throughout space and time. And yet a future Buddha has been prophesized.

I stopped often to catch my breath and make it easy on my unpredictable heart—never sure whether exertion would bring on angina or something far worse. I didn't relish dealing with "an event" in a remote mountain range in Japan. Hiro kept pace with me, and mentioned that he had a heart that beat too fast. I kept my own health hazards secret—no need for unnecessary alarm.

When we finally made it to the top, a life-size statue of a horse greeted our arrival as if Ito-san had traveled with us too. Everyone, it seemed, had come up the mountain with us.

An ancient legend states that Emperor Kazan, after leaving Kokawadera, got lost in the thick forested valleys, and the sound of a galloping horse led him to Sefukuji. Once he arrived at the mountain top temple, he believed that Bato-Kannon, or Horse-headed Kannon had led him to his destination. In gratitude, he commissioned a statue of Bato-Kannon and donated it to the temple. Some believe that the Horse-headed Kannon enshrined in the hondo is the original statue, that it escaped the ravages of time and several fires. A galloping horse cast in bronze stands as a tribute to Emperor Kazan's legendary story.

When the temple priest discovered that two foreigners hiked all the way up the mountain to visit Sefukuji he gave us a private showing of Bato-Kannon. Certainly the dark and blackened carving attested to its age, but whether the Bato Kannon that stood before us was the original remained anyone's guess. For us, the kind hospitality of the priest and his eagerness to share his temple's treasures impressed us more than any relic of the past.

Many statues on the pilgrimage route being "secret" images are either shown once a month, once a year, once every 33 years or not at all. It wasn't the viewing or the not viewing of sacred images that left the strongest impressions, but the friendly faces and feeling of place. Sefukuji, set in a primeval forest on top of a remote mountain in Japan where wandering ascetics practiced for centuries held a powerful presence of an ancient holy site. True to the goeika, "If you can make it to Makinoodera like the pony, your spirits will be lifted." The yearning to return had already crept into my psyche, even though we'd only completed 8 of the 33 temples. Each temple contained long histories, symbolic legends and too many priceless treasures and rare statues to take in, contemplate and absorb with our limited time frame. Details got neglected. Visits went too quickly. Meandering staircases, paths and ancient trails begged to be explored. Images, feelings, thoughts, concerns and practical matters bombarded my senses and sent me into overload. Pending weather fronts kept us moving. With little time for orientation, fine points of rock, ritual or offering got missed. And yet the prospect of making this effort again given the time, expense and difficulty seemed unlikely, which made the visitation of each temple more precious and the nature of our journey fleeting and impressionistic. Each temple would have to be taken in as completely as possible on this our first visit. I would have to be more mindful, more attentive and focused. As in life itself, we got one chance to get it right, to avoid regret, to offer a purposeful contribution of kindness, insight and caring. We didn't get a "do over" only the opportunity to make the most out of each sacred and timeless moment.

I had a choice about whether to complain about the hike up the mountain, or to be grateful that I was still healthy enough to accomplish it. I could whine about the less than perfect weather, or focus on how the lack of sun kept us cool and the lack of rain on this particular day kept the path from getting slippery and dangerous. We always had a choice, and the choices we made mattered. Before we set out on the pilgrimage I stated that the contribution we could make was depositing something positive to the mind stream of consciousness that pervaded space, to essence itself. With our prayers and good intentions to benefit all, we would add to what thousands of pilgrims before and thousands of pilgrims after would contribute to these consecrated domains.

In an interview in Parabola Magazine on the power of pilgrimage, Tara Tulku Rinpoche reminds us that pilgrimage sites become blessed by enlightened minds and this in turn affects all pilgrims who come into the physical vicinity. "It is extremely meritorious to go to the holy sites of any religion," he proclaimed.

Once a temple complex of 80 sub-temples, 3,000 monks, and a place of practice for Shugendo priests and bodhisattvas such as Kobo Daishi, thousands of minds meditating on the dharma for over a thousand years had left their imprints at Sefukuji. The air felt permeated with peaceful, holy thoughts; the mountain itself an abode where Buddhism had been contemplated for centuries. As with all our temple visits, we had to absorb the unabsorbable quickly and intuitively. Early afternoon moved quietly into late afternoon; the sky looked as if it might unleash rain at any minute; Hiro had a long drive back; and we had a long train ride and bus ride to reach our inn back in Kyoto. And so, reluctantly, we descended the mountain, down the steep stone stairs until we reached the entry gate. There we turned and bowed, a bow to acknowledge, in silence, all that Sefukuji represented and all that it had given us.

Hiro-san returned us safe and satisfied to the Izumi City train station. The train would arrive in a few minutes for our trip back to Kyoto. With little time for conversation or reflection, we parted ways with more bows and a heartfelt *Domo arigato gozaiamasu.*

Was that a tear I saw when Hiro said goodbye?

Perhaps it was mine.

Chapter 9

These thoughts
Within my mind
Like six sharp edges —
I pray instead
To make them rounded

Rokkakudo – Temple 18

The Magic of Trees, Flowers and Kannon

Early on in our planning phase, we decided that doing the pilgrimage in a consecutive order would not be practical given several factors: limited time, the cost of transportation, the necessity for good hiking weather at some of the remote temples, and special events scheduled on specific days. In that regard — a very rainy day (not good for hiking) — we jumped from Temple 4 to Temple 18 to partake in the 550th anniversary of the Ikenobo School of Ikebana, the birth place of Japanese ikebana. Two giant shows honored the historical occasion: one located at Takashimiya Department Store; and the other at the school's main headquarters, an eight-story office building with a Starbucks that opens directly into Temple 18 and the Rokkakudo complex.

Ikenobo ikebana, considered the oldest ikebana school in Japan, originated the *tatehana* style of flower arrangement meant to convey the religious feelings of Buddhism. Branches, leaves and flowers placed on temple altars expressed prayers and petitions to the deities — both Shinto and Buddhist. Later, the *rikka* adaptation symbolically represented the entire natural world: mountain peaks, foothills, waterfalls, streams, cliffs, villages and oceans — all imbued with *kami* (nature spirits) and/ or Buddha consciousness.

At Rokkakudo, Buddhism and ikebana had co-existed in one form or another since the 7th century. At that time, Abbot Senmu had returned from his travels to China where he observed flower offerings to Buddha. Upon reflection, he concluded that a "good" flower arrangement should show the relationship between humans and nature and "be harmonized so as to express spiritual vitality." Thus, he established the foundation of ikebana, even though not yet formulated into the styles, rules, and modern expressions we know today.

Senmu also brought to ikebana the trinity, reflected not only in the number and position of flowers, and the traditional altar offerings of incense, candle and flower arrangement, but mirrored in the three jewels of Buddha, Dharma and Sangha. His informal practice of "ikebana" consisted of offering flowers in memory of Rokkakudo founder, Prince Shotoku, said to have been a manifestation of Kannon. Later, Senmu's idea of "three" would be referred to in ikebana arrangements as Heaven, Earth and Man ("Man" being replaced in recent times with the gender neutral "Human"). Some schools cast Heaven as the tallest branch and others (such as Ikenobo) cast Heaven as the middle branch, or horizon, with Human as the tallest.

The present-day headmaster of the Ikenobo School, Sen'ei Ikenobo, when still a young man, explained that, "Very early in Japan's history, a logic was established wherein man and nature were seen as one, wherein the life of a man and the life of a flower were viewed as inseparable." In this way, he expressed a philosophy that contained elements of native Shinto with imported Buddhism and Chinese Confucianism, so intermixed in Japan as to create a unique cultural sensibility and approach to flowers known as Kado: The Way of Flowers.

In *The Master's Book of Ikebana*, Shoka, one of the basic styles of the Ikenobo School, is described thus "...the arrangement starts in earth and reaches toward heaven, and as the branch or flower climbs, it leaves behind its earthly origins and becomes spiritual..."

On the day we visited Rokkakudo and the 550th Anniversary of the Ikenobo School, I brought with me twenty years of ikebana practice steeped in the spiritual philosophy and background of two ikebana traditions: Saga Goryu and Ikenobo. I had more than a casual interest in this fascinating and challenging art form—so much so that I had written a book about it entitled *Heaven and Earth are Flowers: Reflections on Ikebana and Buddhism*. But even though ikebana had been, and still remains, one of my passions, the magnitude of a 550th anniversary show left me dizzy. Admittedly, even though each ikebana arrangement, created with professional skill and elegance, dazzled me with creative use of materials and containers; and even though I knew it took years of practice and study to be able to assemble arrangements of this caliber; and even though I read that some of these arrangements had been executed by the headmaster and headmistress designate (the 46th generation Ikenobo and the first woman to hold that position); and that some of the arrangements, because of their large and complex nature, took several days to complete; the enormity and vastness of human creative expression sent me into stimulation overload, which consequently sent me into pilgrim mode—a good time to take refuge inside the Rokkakudo sanctuary, a six-sided, or hexagon shaped temple, surrounded by modern Kyoto. For an hour or so my sister and I retreated into the formlessness of Being after the dazzle of form had worn us out. Ah, a tranquil respite from the throngs of ikebana enthusiasts, an escape from the thousands who had flocked to the vast exhibition in pouring rain to view the masterfully made arrangements. Men and women, young and old came to express their adoration, and get a taste of the spiritual through works of art. Bless all for their fortitude!

The event, both exhilarating and awe inspiring, competed with the peace and tranquility found at every temple in the middle of this great metropolis—one of the special qualities of Kyoto. The

Rokkakudo, or Chohoji (Dharma Peak Temple), considered the navel of this once ancient capital (symbolically at least) brought us into the very center of the city's special consciousness. The temple contains a smooth round rock with a belly button-like indent and a wish-fulfilling willow tree imbued with a special magic for those seeking an ideal partner.

The Rokkaku willow tree, a species unique to this temple, became associated through ancient legend with the union of Emperor Saga and his princess. To make matters of "coupling" even more prominent at this site, Shinran Shonin, founder of the Jodo Shinshu sect of Buddhism, gave up his vows of celibacy while on retreat here. Kannon, through a visionary dream, directed him to found an order of Buddhism that honored marriage and family.

Now, many centuries later, the lovelorn come to Rokkakudo to hang a paper petition on the Rokkaku Willow hoping that by some divine intervention their soul mate will materialize. Celibacy, although still practiced by a few monks in Japan, has become nearly obsolete. Most monks have wives, and hope to have a son to assume responsibility for the family temple. Nuns, on the other hand, have retained the practice of celibacy. In Japan they have gained equality with the monks, although still rarely inherit a successful temple. Therefore their motivation for becoming ordained differs from monks. Without any financial incentive or family obligation, they take vows to sincerely study the dharma, and to engage in social work to help the community. They learn and preserve traditional Japanese arts, such as tea ceremony and ikebana; and adhere to a strict meditative and study practice within the context of the monastery.

Buddha's original disciples begged to be ordained and live the wandering celibate life, but still he gave instructions for liberation to both ordained and lay practitioners, recognizing that anyone, whether lay or ordained, man or woman, adult or child, had the potential to become enlightened.

Since most of the world still preferred living as couples, once the supposed "ideal mate" was found, a person might ask, how should one be a good Buddhist husband or wife?

In the Pali Cannon, Buddha addresses this issue. While wandering across India, he encounters a group of married couples traveling along the same road. He sits down with them under a shade tree and says, "Householders, there are these four kinds of marriage. A wretch lives together with a wretch; a wretch lives together with a goddess; a god lives together with a wretch; a god lives together with a goddess."

We might all have our own definition (and experience) of a "wretch," but Buddha explained that a wretch "destroys life, takes what is not given, engages in sexual misconduct, speaks falsely, indulges in intoxicants,… is immoral, of bad character, stingy, and abuses and reviles ascetics and Brahmins."

Although the "householder's" life has always been the predominant path for most Buddhists — even more so in today's Western world — Buddha highly praised the ordained celibate life. Celibacy, although not necessarily morally superior, was meant to direct one's focus and energy away from sensual pleasure toward a focused, disciplined life where one could study and contemplate the dharma. Desire for or attachment to others (a partner), had the potential to entrap one in the cyclical nature of life (*samsara*) and therefore be a hindrance to enlightenment.

Not one to follow the norm in most circumstances, I had given up finding, or even desiring, the perfect partner a long time ago. And yet to say "given up" implies a sense of futility, which isn't quite accurate. Suffice it to say, that over the course of many years and many relationships, I saw the error of looking for happiness outside of myself. I had mistakenly thought that if I found the right someone, that I would have a happy fulfilled life. But clearly, thinking that someone else can provide our missing "happy" ingredient is a recipe for disaster. I had to be a goddess before I could find a god, and in that department I had a long way to go. Better to leave well enough alone, and work on my own mind in my own way. Needless to say, I didn't tie a paper petition on the magic willow tree, but I did wish that everyone else who had that inclination (which seemed like most of the world) be and find their own god or goddess.

Apart from wish-fulfilling willow trees, and ikebana inspirations, Rokkakudo housed two stunning statues of Kannon: one a unique rendition of Kannon with a mature grandmotherly face that exuded wise compassion; and the other, a gold thousand-armed version that radiated an extra sweet cosmic expression. I visited Rokkakudo several times during our stay in Kyoto hoping to internalize the essence of these two holy icons. The ikebana show had long gone; and the willow, never lacking in white paper petitions, rustled in the fall air. I continued past it, far more captivated by the statue of thousand-armed Kannon tucked into a back corner of the compound. Her exquisite face filled my camera lens more than once as I tried to capture the essence of her wisdom, that spark of enlightened mind that the artist had striven to express.

Emblazoned upon my mind's eye, a thousand golden arms reached out to all in need, reached out to me, guiding me in complex, mysterious, and yet to be revealed, ways. Even now I can see her welcoming gaze—beckoning from that quiet corner far beyond the willow tree.

Chapter 10

Come again and again
With your pilgrim's heart
To Hasedera
Where the mountains and the vows
Are as deep as the river

Hasedera – Temple 8

Behind the Beauty of Seasons

The small hamlet leading up to Hasedera—one of the most charming on the pilgrimage route—offered an array of goods in shops and stalls lined up and down the narrow hillside street. Various pickled vegetables, bulk beans (mung, garbanzo, large limas...) rice, a special kind of sushi wrapped in a non-edible pungent leaf, and my favorite: manju, a mugwort flavored rice cake filled with sweet bean paste—the best I'd tasted anywhere (I'd tried many).

The animated and friendly vendors, restaurant owners, and inn keepers made for a festive atmosphere that has existed in some form or another going back to the Heian Period. In centuries past, Hasedera, the starting point of the Saigoku Thirty-three Temple Kannon Pilgrimage, not Seigantoji as it is today, emerged as a large and important temple with numerous social, political and religious activities. At that time lords and ladies of the court—including the literary figures, Sei Shonagon and Murasaki Shikibu—journeyed here from the capital for pleasure and sometimes religious reflection. In those days, aristocratic women lived a rather cloistered life inside palace walls hidden from men behind curtains and folding screens. Even when allowed to go on retreat to Buddhist temples, such as Hasedera and Ishiyamadera, the women wore large wide-brimmed hats with veils that prevented others from seeing in. Perhaps on another fall day 1,000 years ago, Sei Shonagon composed the following in her diary, *The Pillow Book:*

> *In autumn, the evenings, when the glittering sun sinks close to the edge of the hills and the crows fly back to their nests in threes and fours and twos; more charming still is a file of wild geese, like specks in the distant sky. When the sun has set, one's heart is moved by the sound of the wind and the hum of the insects.*

And Lady Murasaki, a contemporary of Sei Shonagon, may have elaborated on the love entanglements of Prince Genji, whose sexual exploits sent more than one woman to the nunnery.

But Hasedera existed a couple of centuries well before these two notable Ladies of the Court. Domyo Shonin established a simple hermitage here in 686 AD. From its meager beginnings, Hasedera grew into an important Shingon temple—countless emperors have come and gone, militant monks created havoc here, and fire destroyed this pilgrimage site at least ten times.

When Hasedera burned to the ground in 1052, some thought it marked the third stage of the decline of Buddhism, or "mappo," the final 10,000 years of Buddhist teachings. At the end of this predicted final era of Buddha Shakyamuni, Maitreya, the future Buddha is prophesized to bring pure dharma back to the earth and its beings.

In Japan, the number of Buddhist practitioners has indeed declined (in the same way some Christian denominations have lost parishioners over the years), and in today's world, Hasedera remains on the pilgrimage route perhaps more for its seasonal flower and tree fest than for Buddhism itself. In recent times, priests have established fabulous gardens at their temples to lure in potential devotees. The head priest of Kannonji, and founder of "The 25 Flower Temples of Kansai," said, "...I thought that, rather than pushing people to believe in Buddhism right away, I might be able to encourage them to visit the temple if there were flowers here that they could enjoy. Even if they come first for the flowers, I hope they will gradually be attracted to the tenets of Buddhism."

As an ikebana practitioner I didn't have any quarrel with flowers leading one to greater spiritual dimensions. As the abbot said, "...flowers have tremendous appeal."

At Hasedera—a designated "Flower Temple"—March/April brings forth 1,000 blooming cherry trees; May ushers in 7,000 tree peonies of 150 varieties; and in June 10,000 hydrangeas delight viewers during the rainy season. If that isn't enough, rhododendrons, dogwoods, magnolias and kerria fill in the blooming gaps; and many new pathways and stone retaining walls, surrounding what appeared to be a forthcoming lotus pond, indicated that Hasedera would continue its flower extravaganza into the hottest months of summer. When the lotus blooms wither, brown seed pods loaded with next years plants eject round black marble-like seeds into the muddy ponds. By September grass heads begin forming and by October oatmeal colored plumes begin waving in the wind. The height of autumn (November in Japan) ensures that seasonal magic will continue on even into winter when the stark outline of all those fabulous trees would stand out against snow and blue sky.

We saved Hasadera for a sunny day to saver the delights of the current season: countless red and orange maples and golden gingkoes. Mesmerized by hillsides ablaze with color, we nearly missed the Kannon on view, a 33-foot high, eleven-headed Kannon carved from camphor wood that happens to be the largest wooden Kannon in Japan (listed as a Cultural Property of National Importance). The Hasadera Kannon, unique among Kannons, carries a vase filled with lotus blossoms in her left hand and a Jizo staff in her right. These symbols indicate that Kannon, through her compassion, would and could travel anywhere in the world to heal body and mind, to bring comfort to those suffering from aging, sickness, death, and delusion.

Not to be depressive, but it seemed apt that at the temple known for its dazzling seasonal beauty and allure of colorful "form" that the curtain of illusion be parted to look behind the scenes—or scenery—of life's less glamorous aspects. In the historical story of Prince Siddhartha, we find a young man virtually imprisoned in a pleasure palace by his father so as to keep his precious son from encountering anything resembling suffering. Much like Hasedera, Prince Siddhartha's home, filled with sensual delights, satisfied him for awhile. But like all young men (and women), curiosity about the outside world got the best of him and he snuck outside to see the world. It wasn't long before he encountered an aged person, then a sick person and finally a corpse. These manifest aspects of suffering propelled him to seek a path that led out of suffering.

In the Pali Cannon, Buddha tells the story of the Three Divine Messengers:

A man dies and enters the hell realm where he meets with Lord Yama, the king of death. Lord Yama confronts the man and says, "Didn't you ever see the first divine messenger?"

The man says, no, he did not.

Then Lord Yama describes in great detail a person who is old, bent, shaky and frail.

The man now admits, yes, he did see the first divine messenger, but was negligent.

Then Lord Yama asks the man again whether he saw the second divine messenger. And again the man says no, he did not. And Lord Yama describes in great detail a person who is sick, helpless, feverish and weak.

The man admits, yes, he did see the second divine messenger, but was negligent.

Lastly, Lord Yama asks the man if he saw the third divine messenger, and again the man says, no he did not. And Lord Yama describes in great detail a swollen and bloated corpse.

The man admits that yes, he did see the third divine messenger, but he was negligent.

The story tells of a man who lived a self-absorbed, self-centered life. He didn't have compassion or concern for others. He didn't take responsibility for that which materialized in his life. He didn't pay heed to others' suffering or even his own inevitable impermanence.

Lord Yama pointed out that if we show compassion to others, compassion will also come our way. If we act with kindness, kindness will also come our way. If we have empathy, others will empathize with us. He impresses upon the man that he has no one to blame for the results of his life but himself. He has created everything.

Hasadera represented and presented a glorious sun-filled day brimming with beautiful scenery and mild weather, happy people, good food and fond memories. We celebrated and acknowledged our blessings, knowing that other days would surely come that would present a different face. For awhile, we let ourselves drift into the illusion of maya; the never ending forms and appearances of our existence. We might be dazzled by the promise of thousands of pink peonies—and Kannon loved to offer us nature's bounty—but we, like the man in the story, would also have to confront sickness, aging and death some day.

I tucked these thoughts into a corner of my mind so that I could appreciate—without guilt or trepidation—the bounty manifesting in beautiful ways. Hasadera represented a kind of earthly Pure Land, and whatever it had been in the past—and it had been many things to many kinds of people—it remained an inspirational place where we touched our own beauty through the beauty of leaf, flower and sky. "Come again with your pilgrim's heart," says the goeika. Through peonies, cherry trees, hydrangeas, lotuses, a simple plume of waving grass, the burning red of a perfect maple or the sweet smile of Kannon, the essence of this sacred site will surely lure you in.

Chapter 11

This spring day
At Nan'endo
The radiant brilliance
From Mikasa mountain
Trailing a thin veil of clouds

Nan'endo – Temple 9

Lasso of Compassion

Located in the expansive park-like setting of Kofukuji, complete with 1,200 sacred roaming deer, Nan'endo sits alone and removed like a small octagonal jewel. Inside, and only presented to the public once a year on October 17th, sits Fukukenjaku Kannon, or "Never Empty Lasso" Kannon who carries a long rope to catch sentient beings before they stray too far from the Buddhist path.

By the time we reached Nan'endo by taxi from the Nara train station, we did indeed feel as though we had stepped off the Buddhist path. Already late in the day—and exhausted from a full day at Hasedera—thoughts of afternoon tea and delectable treats at a French bakery in the train station consumed our attention. Historical and culturally significant attributes of the statuary or any feelings of religious devotion paled in comparison. In short, we suffered from a bit of "temple burnout," and foreign travel exhaustion. Escape, comfort and carnal satisfaction enticed. Still, we managed to appreciate the quiet and holy ambience of this temple enclave that has existed in Nara since 669 AD.

The deer, well fed by the thousands of tourists—and therefore nearly tame—still roamed the grounds under ancient temples and one of the tallest five-storied pagodas in Japan. The deer served to remind the pilgrim that a herd of bodhisattvas emanating as deer showed up for Buddha's first dharma talk in

Sarnath; they also symbolized one of Buddha's incarnations, or Jataka Tales, when he took the form of an exceptionally beautiful deer who came to teach the entire human kingdom the meaning of compassion.

The temple priest, friendly and sincerely interested in these two foreigners making the Kannon pilgrimage, revived our pilgrim spirit. By the end of our short visit Nan'endo made a favorable impression and fueled a desire to return someday to view the sacred images. Later, I tried to imagine Kannon's long rope around the specific sufferings of anger, gluttony, addictions and lust said to be the focal points of this particular manifestation, even though, on that particular day, Kannon's lasso could do very little to bring me back to the dharma. But later, when I had time and energy to contemplate the symbolism of Nan'endo, I saw a temple without flowers or maples or stunning waterfalls reflecting octagonal simplicity—in essence Buddhism's Noble Eightfold Path.

The eight points or guidelines of this essential Buddhist teaching are the subtext of the Fourth Noble Truth: the path that leads out of suffering. Right View; Right Intention; Right Speech; Right Action; Right Livelihood; Right Effort; Right Mindfulness; and Right Concentration are the eight stepping stones of that path. If the Buddhist practitioner diligently follows the Eightfold Path with a pure heart enlightenment is nearly guaranteed.

And yet anyone who has attempted to follow even one of these "Rights"—let's say, Right Speech—knows the difficulty. Right Speech encompasses telling the truth (not only to others but also to ourselves), refraining from gossip, slander and idle chatter; abstaining from harsh words, shouting or yelling out of anger, and engaging in sarcasm.

Idle chatter seemed harmless enough, but some texts defined "chatter" as watching mindless television shows, reading sensational news stories or watching R rated films known for sex, violence and harsh language. Rather, by following Right

Speech we wanted to utilize our precious human life to promote positive feelings towards others, to create harmony, friendship, cooperation and value. In following Right Speech, the pilgrim could practice mindfulness regarding all her interactions with train conductors, taxi drivers, ticket vendors, priests and other pilgrims. The pilgrim always had a choice to be friendly, courteous and respectful, or sullen, pushy and demanding. We've all experienced both kinds of behavior and felt the impact of both positive and negative speech.

Right View allows us to investigate the spiritual path and come to an understanding that, yes indeed, we can see the importance and benefit of following precepts and cultivating wisdom and compassion. We see the benefit to ourselves, others, our community and society if we accept and practice all the other "Rights" as a path to liberation.

But Kannon knows that even though we've seen the wisdom of this path that it is easy to stray. That's when the lasso comes out in the form of inspiration: a friend's comment, a book, a talk, a walk in the mountains, a disaster or death—anything that will bring us back to the dharma and our journey toward our spiritual home. With Right Effort, we give it another go, maintain our faith, return to the meditation cushion, go on a retreat, anything to keep us engaged in discovering truth, in waking up.

In Right Effort we employ Right Mindfulness, stay in the present moment aware of body, speech and mind; aware of others, awake to what's needed now, cognizant of our habitual tendencies and mistaken views.

Perhaps we see that our way of making a living is not Right; it violates our sense of ethics; it compromises our integrity; it harms other beings (humans, animals or plants); it harms our self with too much stress and no satisfaction; we're robbed of time for contemplation, inquiry or meditative retreat; our job takes us away from our family which causes alienation and discord. Once again Kannon throws her lasso so we can reassess our situation, so we can practice Right Livelihood.

On the day of our visit, we had let Right Intention be waylaid by fatigue, cravings, and Wrong View. Our only practice of Right Intention manifested in keeping our vow to participate in the pilgrim rituals by remembering to purify, make prayers, offer incense and give thanks. We performed Right Action, but perhaps lacked Right View.

It is said that if we practice the first seven "Rights" then the final one, Right Concentration, will empower our meditations, help us stay focused on our object and allow us to penetrate to the truth of emptiness: the absence of inherent existence.

The octagonal design of Nan'endo reminded me through sacred geometry of Buddha's Way. Like so many symbols along the pilgrimage route that pointed, in one way or another, to the path of liberation, the number eight, in its holistic implication exhibited yet another facet of the finger pointing at the moon. If the number eight failed to shake us out of our mundane dream-sleep then Kannon's thousand arms might bring us back to the Way, or perhaps her sweet smile, motherly gaze, rays of light, sacred implements or holy lasso would create a spark of remembrance.

Ah, yes, Buddha's Way—surely something to contemplate over tea and pastries at a boulangerie.

Chapter 12

Placing the rocks
Adding flowing water
Tsubosaka's
Sand garden
Becomes the Pure Land

Tsubosakadera – Temple 6

Big Buddha Jataka Tales

The head of a giant Buddha towering above gray roof tiles was our first glimpse of Tsuboskadera. More giant Buddhas emerged and multiplied as we began to tour the grounds. The Buddhas got bigger and bigger and bigger; the biggest being a white, 360-foot, 500-ton statue of Kannon that looked out over layers of mountains and valleys like a mountain herself: grand, all encompassing and powerful. At her feet lay Buddha Shakyamuni in the reclining pose of entering Nirvana, that state of supreme stillness where all desires, attachments, niggling worries, fears, delusions and negative states of mind have been eradicated.

Getting to Tsubosakadera from Kyoto proved to be the antithesis of nirvana—nearly half a day by express train, then local train, and finally a 40-minute bus ride up a steep and narrow mountain road before the Southern Temple of the Dharma Lotus came into view. But the sunny autumn day, with red-leaved maples and white Buddhas and bodhisattvas imprinted against blue sky soon transported our spirits to a pilgrim's Pure Land. Temple 6, like a Wonderland painted by the Picturesque Temple Kami, erased all memories of our transportation travails. How quickly circumstances and emotions changed—the forever impermanence of form, thought, and feeling playing out like an endless film strip. Except for a handful of plein air watercolorists stationed at prominent points around the compound, we had the place nearly to ourselves.

Besides its physical beauty, Tsubosakadera's long history of healing eye diseases and correcting vision problems explained the pile of glasses mounding up at the base of the hondo—although my skeptical self provided another version of how those glasses got there. Still, I silently made a half-hearted prayer for perfect vision, even though, truth be told, I didn't mind wearing glasses; and I didn't expect any miracles, at least not of the physical kind—although some assistance in correcting my *inner* vision would be welcome. In that respect the mammoth Buddhas began to have an impact.

Some pilgrims (who will remain nameless) aren't particularly fond of gigantic Buddhas—and I had to agree that from an artistic point of view the smaller, older statues of Kannon captured a feminine sweetness not found in Great Kannon. But Great Kannon had a power akin to a giant redwood, cedar, or sequoia: colossal objects that filled the sky with an unmistakable presence. Seemingly indestructible and eternal I imagined these larger than life images lasting for thousands of years (although perhaps a foolish idea in this earthquake prone country). The Great Kannons, meant to fill one with awe—which for me they did—also left a lingering feeling that Buddha consciousness resided everywhere and in all directions: above the trees, over the mountains, across the valleys, into the seas and throughout the galaxy. Kannon's *Karana* hand mudra, meant to dispel negative energy and disease, emanated invisible lazar beams into the cosmos—or so I imagined. Great Kannon, a real tangible force, appeared as a different personality from her more esoteric sisters. Yet all of them blessed the onlooker in a myriad of ways.

As a symbol that works directly on the subconscious mind, Buddha and bodhisattva images can be quite powerful in evoking peace, awakened mind, compassion, wisdom, inner serenity, all pervasive knowing... to name a few. Just like Amida Buddha—

representative of the formless state—so too Buddha Shakyamuni and Kannon indicate a world or universal element that cannot be seen, but only felt, only pointed to. Icons tell us of another deeper reality. They take us inward. Kannon in particular evokes the compassionate mind, the Mahayana path of service to others, of foregoing nirvana until everyone is liberated. Buddha Shakyamuni on the other hand symbolizes not only the universal qualities of wisdom and compassion, but the ordinary qualities of being a human being. A historical figure who lived 2,500 years ago in India, Buddha Shakyamuni came to show humans how to become enlightened in a physical body.

At Tsubosakadera, large stone relief panels depict the final life story of Buddha Shakyamuni. Although in total 547 "birth stories" make up a body of teachings called the Jataka Tales—dramatizations of the Buddha's lives leading up to and including his enlightenment—Tsubosakadera showcases scenes from Buddha Shakyamuni's last life, where he finally becomes, well... the Buddha.

Buddha's final incarnation on the wheel of samsara or cyclic existence began with a magical birth in Lumbini Grove, where it is said that flower petals rained down from the sky. He grew up as Prince Siddhartha in a great palace, got married, had a child and lived the privileged life until the day he went into the village and encountered an old person hobbling along in pain; then a person with an incurable disease lying by the side of the road; and finally a corpse being cremated on a funeral pyre. Distraught and saddened at the scale of human misery, he vowed to find a way out of suffering. Even though he had a wife and child, searching for an antidote to the torment of the human condition became his priority. He left his young family, left the cushy prince life, left all the pleasures of the aristocracy and joined a band of wandering ascetics. For six years he lived on little to eat, depriving his body and mind of all sensory experiences. But enlightenment evaded him and he became

73

weak and malnourished. Then one day a young woman came by and offered him a sip of rice porridge. He took a drink—several drinks—and began to feel stronger. He realized that living a life of extreme deprivation did not produce results, and thus declared the Middle Way. Conjuring great effort, he resolved to sit in meditation under the bodhi tree until he saw the Truth. Mara, the one who tempts with sensory delight, came around to derail the bodhisattva's effort, but even though he sent every conceivable temptation his way, the great bodhisattva—soon to be Buddha—remained steadfast in his meditation. Mara demanded to know how he could resist being seduced by all the delights of the world. The bodhisattva proclaimed that by practicing the Ten Perfections for untold eons, the way had been prepared.

Mara turned away in disgust and at that moment the Buddha touched the earth so that She could bear witness to the full truth of his Awakening. For the next 45 years Buddha taught the dharma to his disciples until his final passing into nirvana at the time of his death.

Buddha's 546 previous lives, stories meant to teach about all the trials and tribulations of his evolution to full awakening, show how the Ten Perfections or *Paramitas* of Generosity, Virtuousness, Renunciation, Wisdom, Effort, Patience, Truthfulness, Resolve, Loving-Kindness and Equanimity bring ultimate liberation. Utilizing these very same attributes, the monks at Tsubosakadera, committed to helping the blind and those with Hansen's disease in India, fulfill their own Jataka legacy.

According to the greater message of Buddhist teachings, we too must cultivate these Paramitas as each of us, like Prince Siddhartha, is meant to follow the path of the bodhisattva to our final destination: Buddhahood. Our life—or lives—makes up our unique Jataka Tale, with our own challenges to face, grapple with and rise above. How many lives will it take? Many, or only one? No one knows.

Even nations travel the evolutionary path of karmic evolution. Will we collectively express Loving-Kindness to all people? Will we be generous with our resources? Truthful in our work? Compassionate to ourself and others? Everything we do personally, in our communities, and our nations will create future causes and conditions. It's up to us. What kind of world do we want to create?

Practicing the Ten Perfections, as dramatized by the Jataka Tales, polishes the rough edges of our being so that the diamond light of Buddha consciousness can finally be seen. These stories, the spiritual theater of ancient days, dramatized human evolution and impressed upon audiences of old the importance of cultivating virtuous states of mind. Each story tells a three-dimensional tale in living color, a tale meant to entertain, teach, remember and pass along.

I viewed my own life story—although much less dramatic than the Jataka Tales— as one opportunity after another to either do the right thing or not, live with integrity or not, be kind and compassionate or not, be generous or not. We had, at every moment, the opportunity to live our lives with Big Buddha Mind… or not.

Chapter 13

In the morning when I see
The dew on the moss
In the garden of Okadera
It looks just like lapis
Shining brightly

Okadera – Temple 7

The Five Wisdom Buddhas

An old Shingon compound set deep into the side of a mountain, Temple 7, darkened by afternoon shadows and thick foliage, possessed some noteworthy symbols that left profound reverberations. Colorful banners in white, yellow, red, blue, and green hanging from the main temple's veranda lit up the otherwise cheerless compound. The colors' symbolic meanings vary in different parts of the world, but in the Shingon sect of Okadera, they represent the Five Wisdom Buddhas (*Godai Nyorai*) of Vajrayana Buddhism.

These Five Buddhas, represented by the elements of space, air, fire, earth and water, form a mandala with the Cosmic Buddha, or *Dainichi Nyorai*, in the center. The colors represent aspects of Buddha-nature. White, for example, stands for the Cosmic Buddha, and in the Cosmic Buddha philosophy, all phenomena emanate from the One, and the One represents the unity of All. Dainichi Nyorai, associated with the element of space, and the sense perception of sight, transforms ignorance into wisdom. Cosmic Buddha is no other than *Amaterasu*, the Shinto sun goddess of the universe and the supreme creator in Japan's native religion.

Blue represents Ashuku Buddha, the earth element found in the east who rules the sense perception of sound. He transforms anger and irritation into compassion for others.

Yellow indicates Hosho Buddha, the fire element found in the south, who rules over the sense perception of smell. He teaches equanimity and self-control while dispelling arrogance, greed and self-indulgence. We remember that all living beings are equal, no one being superior or inferior; we are all Buddhas in a state of individual and collective evolution, and at the same time whole and complete.

Red stands for Amida Buddha, including Kannon his attendant, the water element found in the west who rules over the sense perception of taste. He transforms desire and passion into the wisdom of discriminating awareness and non-attachment.

Green represents Fukujoju Buddha, the equivalent of Green Tara in Tibetan Buddhism, the air element in the north. This Buddha's energy compels us to follow the bodhisattva's path and transforms jealousy and envy into acts of kindness and generosity.

Everyone and everything, said to be a mix of all the colors or energies and their opposites — wisdom and ignorance, male and female, peaceful and wrathful, north and south, east and west — are entangled and contained within this system. Together, the Wisdom Buddhas portray a holistic view of Ultimate Truth. The colors, elements and symbols point to an energy system of enlightened and wrathful action, which explains the legend of the dragon said to reside in Okadera's pond.

Long ago a dragon with both destructive and constructive characteristics lived in the mountains and valleys near Okdadera. At times the dragon created so much rain that floods destroyed crops and towns. At other times, the shamans called upon the dragon's power to eliminate drought. In order to harness the dragon's energy the founding shaman priest of Okadera managed to subdue and coax the dragon into the temple's pond. He then covered the pond with a giant stone engraved with the Sanskrit "A" syllable (pronounced "Ah"). The "A" syllable in

Shingon philosophy, described as "the basis of all words, the mother of all syllables, and the wellspring of all teachings... a metaphor for all pervading enlightenment," indicates the power of one sound, one esoteric seed. Simply seeing or hearing the letter "A" can induce instant awakening.

This was no ordinary dragon! In times of drought, (physical drought or spiritual drought?) the monks removed the lid (to release the power present within our own deep "pond" of Being?). Shingon practitioners meditate on an "A" syllable inside a moon disc. The visualization, meant to produce the brightness (like the moon) of awakened consciousness—Buddha mind—leads to enlightenment.

The dragon story of Okadera, an ancient allegory meant for a general population less schooled in the esoteric teachings of Shingon Buddhism, points to complex "secret" teachings—*Mikkyo*, in Japanese—only available to the initiated. The monks and nuns who take Shingon Buddhist vows and study under the guidance of a master receive special teachings through oral transmission—a common practice in other spiritual/artistic traditions in Japan such as tea ceremony, Noh theater, court poetry and flower arranging.

Like the dragon imprisoned in the pond of our own subconscious mind, we can send out loving, helpful, sensitive, generous and healing vibes, or judgmental, rude, domineering, stingy and destructive vibes—transformative potential lies dormant but ready to be activated.

The banners, like all religious symbols, and especially symbols found in Japanese culture, merely hint at layers of meaning. The Shingon practices of meditation, rituals and visualizations bring one closer to actual realization or a personal experience of True Self in this very life, not, as some Buddhist teachings propound, after eons of lives.

Kukai (a.k.a. Kobo Daishi), the founder of Shingon Buddhism, laid out a complex system of innumerable levels of consciousness, all of them stages in the process of complete awakening. The Shingon teachings can be heady and complex, but the colorful banners prompt one to remember the Wisdom Buddhas and the energy systems they represent. The banners point to the positive and life affirming reality of the spiritual life, and what Tibetan Buddhists call "the enlightened wisdom of our emotions."

In the shadowy darkness of Okadera's landscape, the banners of wisdom energy blazed under the autumn sun with more intensity. Beyond them, toward the mountain side, a path meandered deep into the forest and up to a cave, or inner sanctuary that opened into the deep earth. Womb-like, primordial, something about the cave exuded a foreboding energy, or perhaps an unfamiliar energy. I felt attracted and repelled at the same time. The cave had an ancient, otherworldly feeling; and indeed Okadera had been born in the days of clans, shamans and wandering ascetics going back 1,300 years.

The area around the cave, dark and damp with the sound of trickling water coming from some unknown place, evoked an eerie presence. So too the moss-covered white stone Buddha half buried into the embankment that appeared to have sprung from the earth itself.

By late afternoon a chill had settled in. I felt compelled to return to the warmth of the sun and the wisdom energies. The path meandered up and around a hillside planted with over 3,000 rhododendrons, numerous azaleas and tree peonies, all of which put Okadera on the "Flower Temples Pilgrimage" circuit. But more than its spring flower fest, Okadera, known as "the oldest holy place in Japan to provide protection against evil," conjured images of unspeakable acts committed in moments of darkness, the darkest most ignorant side of human nature, even though pilgrims at Okadera thought mostly of the "evil" of Mother Nature and natural disaster, the unpredictable personality of dragon. Pilgrims offered prayers here to avert disaster in whatever form it might show up: illness, accident, earthquake, tsunami...

Having said our own prayers, we readied to leave Okadera. In so doing we passed oatmeal colored pampas grass bowing elegantly in front of gray and tan walls, a perfect Japanese design motif that appears in woodblock prints, incense holders, textiles... I paused to appreciate this emblem of autumn, depicted like all other plants and trees in Japan as seasonal indicators and wonders of the natural world. A haiku by Issa captured the moment:

> *the plume of the pampas grass —*
> *the helpless tremblings*
> *of a lonely heart*

My "lonely heart" wasn't brought on by an absence of others, or a need for someone to fill a void, but a yearning to know, to experience what all the Buddhist symbols pointed to. Whether wisdom banners, symbolic dragon energy, or the purity and humble impermanence of nature itself, all phenomena appeared as teachers, sign posts, and maps that kept saying: *This way*: the finger pointing at the moon, until somehow via divine space shuttle, we made a lunar landing—home at last.

Fleeting impressions leave residues to be examined later. Those gathered at Okadera were no exception. I felt an esoteric resonance beating like an ancient heart, a heart still beating at all the temples on the Kannon route—a pilgrimage that had called to me from across a great ocean, and had me following the trail of symbols on this ancient devotional path.

And yet, at the end of the day, with all of those sensory perceptions imprinted and yet to be unraveled, the task at hand was merely finding a bus stop somewhere in the vicinity of this dragon realm.

Chapter 14

Looking at this flower
My wish now
Is that the thousand flowers
In Kodo's garden
Will bloom

Kodo (Gyoganji) – Temple 19

Benzaiten's Blessing

Benzaiten, the goddess of everything that flows—water, music, knowledge, art, song, dance, and poetry—intrigued me as much as Kannon. At Kodo, Temple 19, her own special shrine, tucked into a corner of this small but delightful inner city compound, honors her poetic presence.

A Tendai temple, and the only one on the Saigoku Pilgrimage operated by nuns, Kodo is also the only temple that doesn't have any commercial enterprise—not one souvenir for sale on the premises. Ironically, this sweet little neighborhood temple sits in the heart of Kyoto right off of Teramachi-dori, a famous shopping street known for tea utensils, woodblock prints, antique ceramics, French pastries, and a vast shopping arcade.

When one steps off that street, enters Kodo through its front gate—known here as "Medicine Gate"—and gets a taste of the spiritual healing contained in this non-descript little corner of Kyoto, the allure of material goods soon fades into irrelevance— at least for a little while. Fresh, bright flowers that adorn the temizuya look as if grown in someone's garden rather than purchased at the florist; the grounds are sparse but kept clean and tidy; the icons beckon with serene smiles and esoteric hand mudras; calm and quiet soon replace the city's hubbub.

The most prominent statuary at Kodo, other than Benzaiten,

but also including her, consists of the Seven Gods of Good Fortune who bestow the virtues of long life, prosperity, recognition, honesty, kindness, self-esteem and generosity—qualities taught in the *Benevolent Kings Perfection of Wisdom Sutra*, a wisdom sutra for protection of the nation. Depicted as arriving by Treasure Ship on New Year's Eve, the Seven Gods bring happiness to sentient beings, especially if a favorable dream enters your sleep on New Year's Eve.

But Temple 19 had more than Seven Gods and a beautiful Benzaiten statue; Kodo had a real living Benzaiten disguised as a nun.

When we presented our pilgrim books to the temple steward at the nokyo, the elderly nun sitting next to her wanted to know where we were from. She wanted to shake our hand—an odd request in a country where bowing is the norm and hand-shaking rarely initiated. Delighted to comply, especially to a wizened grandmotherly Buddhist with loving-kindness emanating from her smile, I extended my ungloved cold hand. When she felt the coldness, she held on a moment longer—also unusual in a country where handshakes are brief and limp, never lingering— with the admonition to take care. She rubbed my hand between both of her very warm hands, which warmed my heart in equal measure—and perhaps more.

That night I had an intense dream. Nothing remains of the specific details other than a memory of being filled with profound and exquisite bliss. When I awoke the next morning, the memory of the old nun rubbing my hand seemed uncannily connected. I wondered if some exchange had happened on an energetic level—a transmission of some kind?

In Sanskrit, the word *shaktipat* means to confer spiritual energy to another; a psychic transmission from guru to disciple, or an enlightened person to someone receptive. The transmission can be imparted through various means, such as a word, a look, or a touch. The recipient cannot be forced or coerced to receive the transmission, but if he/she is open and willing the divine energy can enter to assist the seeker in awakening.

The blissful dream (a Kannon connection perhaps?) wasn't the only event that made me pause to reflect on the potential blessings of our pilgrimage. The day after our trip to Okadera, on a busy afternoon in downtown Kyoto, Gwen and I stopped at a crosswalk and waited for the light to change. We were talking and somewhat distracted. The light turned green. I moved forward to step off the curb. In the next second something made me hesitate. I instinctively put my hand in front of Gwen, and said, "Watch out." In that moment, a taxi, traveling at break neck speed, came careening around the corner from seemingly nowhere; it squealed through the crosswalk. One more step and both of us would have been flung through the air like rag dolls. Before the next tick of the timeless clock, the speeding taxi had disappeared from sight. The convergence of events had come and gone in a kind of dream state that left an impression and a question about the mystery of lives unfolding. Hadn't we just visited the temple where pilgrims pray to avert disaster?

Whether by some divine intervention or random luck, the erasure of negative karma or the accumulation of merit, our pilgrimage *did* continue under an umbrella of blessings. Over time, the stream of steady good fortune and synchronicity started to erode residual skepticism. I trusted that the power behind our pilgrim's intentions wove a kind of sacred web around these two wandering women. Something extraordinary felt emergent.

At the same time, I knew that the universe liked to surprise when things got too comfortable—the razor's edge of walking the path of human existence. One had to always remain open to anything and everything, to expect the unexpected, to embrace the moving river of forms appearing and disappearing and events arising and falling.

Chapter 15

All night long
As the moon shines down
On Mimuroto,
Along the rapids of Uji River
White waves are rising.

Mimurotoji - Temple 10

The Beautiful Face of Kannon

Built on a hillside overlooking Uji—the tea capital of Japan and Heian Period pilgrimage route—Temple 10 surprised us with beautiful botanical gardens, ponds, stunning fall maples, and gingkos. This temple compound had something to dazzle the weary pilgrim no matter what time of year: 20,000 azaleas cascading down the entire length of the mountain side in April and May; the sky-like purity of blue hydrangea in June; sacred lotuses bursting from dozens of Chinese ceramic pots in July and August; and scarlet maples that created a lacy filigreed forefront to the spectacular vermillion pagoda in November. One of the "Flower Temples," Mimurotoji made our growing list of "must come back in spring."

Several temple compounds along the Kannon route had been transformed throughout the years into spectacular gardens replete with unimaginable collections of flowers, shrubs and trees. "Nature," had always played a part in spiritual matters; its special connection with Buddhism began with Buddha Shakyamuni when he proclaimed: "Together with me the Great Earth, all beings have become enlightened. The grass, the trees, the very soil have achieved Buddhahood." Nothing got left out of the awakened state, and everything reflected it. The Buddha called upon the earth to bear witness to the Truth, and the earth roared "I bear you witness!" With that, the Buddha awakened to his true nature and is now portrayed with his right hand in the mudra of pointing to, or "touching" the earth. Since that time, many prominent figures in Buddhism's development in Japan — monks such as Saigyo, Kobo Daishi and Dogen — expressed a profound connection with nature.

Saigyo, a Buddhist monk famous for his poetry and love of nature, lived during the end of the Heian Period and beginning of the Kamakura Period, an era shortly after the beginning of Mappo (1052) the predicted decline of Buddhism. In *Japanese Pilgrimage,* the author Oliver Statler states: "To Saigyo nature did not exist as the creation of god; nature was not a symbol of the Buddha, not something through which one might approach the Buddha, not an aid to comprehending the power and majesty of the Buddha — nature *was* Buddha." Saigyo reveled in nature and went on to say that, "...being in nature — being alone in nature, open to it, vulnerable to it — was a religious act."

To forget the self and "merge," so to speak, with nature, without any feeling of separation, without a sense of "out there" and "in here," could momentarily appear when least expected and just as quickly vanish. Arising unbidden, the "separate self" or ego mind, insisted on intruding. Whenever the veil began to lift and expose a greater reality that old worn out mind of ignorance rose to the surface.

In the *Shobogenzo,* or *Treasury of the True Dharma Eye,* a compilation of Zen teachings written by Dogen Zenji, founder of Soto Zen, we find:

The grass, trees and the forest are also transient. Thus they are no other than Buddha-nature. People and things, body and mind are transient. Thus they are Buddha-nature. The land, mountains and rivers are transient. Therefore they are Buddha-nature. These mountains and rivers and this land are all the sea of Buddha-nature... To see mountains and rivers is to see Buddha-nature.

Mimurotoji's gardens, symbolic of the greater wild world of Dogen's "mountains and rivers" brought me into this sphere of transience. Not a temple strong in icons, or legends that pointed to a hidden Buddhist story, rather Temple 10 embodied the magic of nature, another face of Kannon and the Awakened Mind we call Buddha.

People came here to celebrate nature, to revel in it, to be reminded of their own inner beauty and spiritual essence. Nature could do that better than anything I knew; it called forth our inner world so we could bathe in its splendor for a little while. Although this awakened clear mind, the "sun" of our own inner essence, was available everywhere and at all times, we often failed to recognize it. Being in the presence of nature, of beauty, ignited a spark of remembrance. The holy quality of walking among flowers, frolicking under leafy trees and allowing ourselves to be carried away by a trickling stream flowing over smooth stones helped us forget, for a little while, all the fears and anxieties that kept our mind distracted from True Self. The beauty of nature made us drop our petty distractions so that the clarity and happiness of our innate beauty could catch us unaware.

Kobo Daishi, along with many who came before and after, felt the closeness of Buddha-nature more readily in remote places: mountains, caves and primeval forests. He built his sacred Buddhist community atop Mt. Koya, surrounded by eight peaks representing the eight petals of a lotus. Mountains in Japan, once thought to be the home of the gods and therefore off limits to humans, eventually became sanctuaries where, first men, and much later women, could touch those "gods" with their very being. According to the *Sakuteiki*, the oldest manual on garden making in Japan, even stones had spirit and symbol, and in the Buddhist tradition represented deities such as Fudo Myoo. When one laid eyes on such stones, particularly those in and around waterfalls, the aspiration to seek enlightenment was said to be activated.

Although Mimurotoji has various animal totems—rabbit, snake, bull—that purportedly grant particular healings, the beauty of its gardens held the most potential for satisfying the pilgrim's core yearning. The natural feminine energy of the Mimurotoji grounds reflects Kannon's heart. Go here to open to her wonders, experience her in a flower, leaf or stone, to deepen your understanding of the transient nature of all phenomena.

Chapter 16

Although heavy
The five sins
Will not be in the world
When I go to pray
At Rokuhara temple

Rokuharamitsuji – Temple 17

Kuya and the Eleven Heads of Kannon

Another neighborhood temple in a narrow back street of Kyoto, Temple 17 had two stunning statues that contributed to the many Buddhist layers of meaning: one depicted the monk Kuya with six tiny Amida Buddha figures emanating from his mouth; and the other, a modern jet black statue of Eleven-headed Kannon positioned directly in front of the entry gate, had scholars speculating over its meaning.

One explanation for Kannon's eleven heads states that Kannon took in all the profound suffering of the world and became so distraught that her head split into eleven pieces. But how does the "sheer shock" hypothesis—although understandable given the suffering of the world—explain the laughing head at the back?

Another explanation for Eleven-headed Kannon posits that she is directing her gaze into the ten directions, or quarters, of the universe. This idea supports the omnipresent aspect of Kannon's wisdom and compassion whereby she sees what is needed and where, and manifests an appropriate form.

The most probable explanation for Kannon's eleven heads involves the Shingon teaching of the ten levels of mind and the bodhisattva path, a progressive path in which the eleventh head, final Buddhahood, is represented by Amida Buddha. The heads, like many Buddhist "sign posts," say, *This Way. See!*

In Taiko Yamasaki's *Shingon: Japanese Esoteric Buddhism,* everyone, whether in this life or a previous one, starts out with a "Goatish Mind," defined as a mind of total ignorance that only cares about satisfying desires and cravings before realizing that maybe there's a bit more to life than physical indulgence. One then adopts a set of ethics. Although still of a "Foolish Mind," this mind eventually leads to wanting a peaceful dwelling place after death—heaven perhaps—and a god or deity who will look after you and protect you from harm: "The Childlike Mind." After a time, maybe by following a spiritual path that purports to lead to heaven (or a Pure Land), you start to question this dogma and discover that the "self" who yearns for a loving divine mother-father figure is not as permanent and "real" as once thought; and yet the relative world still seems pretty solid. By now you've progressed from a level one state of mind to a level four. A breakthrough might take you to the fifth level of mind whereby you see the emptiness of all phenomena, even though you have not yet gained compassion for all sentient beings. After more years of meditating your mind wakes up to the "Compassionate Mahayana Mind," but you are only at the sixth level and have four more to go. To get to the top you must realize the emptiness of objects within the mind and the mind itself, and move on to seeing that "the worlds of delusion and enlightenment, the worlds of matter and mind, the human world, and all possible worlds, are contained in a single thought within the individual mind."

It would seem that if we could get to and hold this level-eight state of mind, entitled "The Mind of the Single Way of Truth," we'd have reached "home." But, according to Shingon doctrine, we have two stages to go: "The Mind of Ultimate No-Self Nature," and "The Secret, Sublime Mind." The ninth mind reveals that "all things interpenetrate" and "all things contain eternal truth," but the tenth mind "fully realizes its true nature...

the creative mind at the source of all things." The eleventh mind (or head) signifies the culmination of the ten levels of mind. You are now Amida Buddha (*Amitabha* in Sanskrit): The Buddha of Infinite Light.

The monk Kuya, founder of Rokuharamitsuji, clearly exhibited through his actions, the sixth level, "The Compassionate Mahayana Mind." And perhaps he went all the way to number ten, which might explain why he is depicted in statue form with tiny Amida Buddhas emanating from his mouth—signifying the wisdom and purity of every word he uttered or chanted.

Kuya traveled throughout Japan teaching Buddhism through dance while reciting the *Nembutsu* mantra. He built wells, roads and bridges for people in poor villages. In Kyoto he buried and offered prayers for the dead who were dumped at Rokuharamitsuji because they couldn't afford a proper burial. Like a 10th-century Mother Teresa, he lived a simple life, worked tirelessly to help those without privilege, and administered to the sick, dying and dead. But his legacy did not continue at Rokuharamitsuji. After Kuya's death this once simple temple evolved into a vast complex with over 5,000 residents. In the 12th century, during one of Japan's many clan wars, the Rokuharamitsuji community met its demise. Eventually, over the centuries, it reverted back to a simple neighborhood temple, but this time more a repository of artistic statuary than a mission of mercy.

The friendly monk stamping everyone's pilgrim book seemed surprised but pleased to see two foreigners standing in line. He complimented us for using a few Japanese words; and then, to acknowledge our endeavor, gave us each a special prayer card. In that moment, as in many during our time in Japan, I experienced the frustration of "language barrier." Any possibility of an in-depth meaningful conversation with the monk on religious or philosophical matters was out of the question. Yet something of our spirits, unspoken but perceived, communicated without words; it had to suffice.

Most people—including myself—fail to realize the impact that actions, subtleties and simple gestures can have during a brief encounter. No matter how seemingly short or unimportant my interaction with a stranger (especially a foreigner) I often forget that the impression and imprint has the potential to linger for days and weeks and perhaps even a life time. If we make the best of every opportunity we can fill the universe with blessings rather than hate, bigotry and divisiveness. The "Goatish Mind" and "Foolish Mind," minds focused on self rather than others, can and must be transcended if we are to progress as a species.

With Kannon's eleven heads of awakening and Kuya's work, values and presence bubbling out of Temple 17, I thought of my own path with its pitiful accomplishments—realizations that hovered somewhere between level one and four, with intermittent glimpses—very briefly—of levels five; and maybe, on a good retreat day, a level six. Even in contemplating the remainder of our Part I pilgrimage, I had sunk into a lower level mind of worry and fear. We had four temples remaining with the most difficult—in terms of physical difficulty—our last. Rather than reposing in a higher level of spiritual realization, say a level seven, whereby one realizes the empty nature of thought, I worried about my heart, my stamina and the weather. Now the end of November, snow in the mountains was possible.

To counter my nagging anxious mind, I conjured the reassuring voice of my internal Kannon-sama—my personal dragon—who stood up to fear, told me to stay in the present moment, and be as physically prepared with food, water and proper clothing as I could. That same voice also reminded me that Sefukuji, the most difficult to reach of all temples so far, had also been the most satisfying and rewarding of ventures. Would Kami Daigoji, the last temple on this trip, be the same? Or would disaster finally catch up with us?

Gwen entertained similar worries but for different reasons. Her old foot injury had been aggravated by our previous hikes up and down stone staircases. Kami Daigoji promised to be the ultimate challenge for her as well. The constant reminder of the limitations of an aging body forced me to contemplate once again my own impermanence. Unless I died from an accident—such as from the speeding taxi that ran a red light—I would perhaps someday have to confront the loss of mobility: the ability to hike, travel, even walk perhaps. We'd seen it with our parents: our mother's partial paralysis after several small strokes, her inability to garden or even water the plants on her patio, her inability to cook, drive, do laundry, or even get herself to the bathroom at times. Our father too eventually lost the capacity to go up and down stairs, to drive, or even comb his hair, which is why at 90 he got his first buzz cut. So instead of experiencing the blissful rapture of the emptiness of all existence, I got stuck on, *How does one prepare for this inevitable decline of the body?* The ego did not like it one bit, so of course the ego had to be subdued. Better to identify with formlessness rather than form, to feel a Beingness that has no boundaries or limits. The sound of a crow cawing in the misty mountains or the bell ringing at the temple gate had far more enduring possibilities. The candle flame flickering on the shrine, the incense smoke reaching upward with prayers and devotion—these too had deeper resonance. The water trickling from the dragon's mouth, the purifying and washing away of delusion—much more satisfying than focusing on a body that would perish just as surely as the red maple leaves fluttering to the ground—even the ones we savored and preserved in our notebooks. Perhaps in the same way that the autumn display of color dazzled my senses and made my heart joyful, I could learn to cherish this cycle of change and impermanence. I too might learn how to depart gracefully like the leaves that floated to the ground without a care. Why not be a weathered piece of wood or a lichen-covered branch, a stone worn smooth or a perfect red maple leaf with spots and brown tips. Why confer a judgment or repulsion upon myself that I would never think to bestow upon a plant. Didn't the ikebana artist show the beauty of a yellowing decaying leaf in her arrangement? Wasn't that leaf stunning against the purple orchid or clematis held high by an earthenware vase?

Whenever I shed this "overcoat" of a body and proceed to my next destination, I hope to have gained some insight beyond the needs of mundane concerns. Life and death perceived in the ordinary sense, at level one or two—physical matter that only existed for pleasure, safety and security and then died alone and poor—surely created a sense of sorrow. Better to strive for that tenth stage of mind now in this very life, while I still had one. This echoed the Shingon way: to achieve enlightenment in this very life, in this very body.

But honestly, on most days I identified with the Kannon head that expressed surprise, shock and sadness. Or, at times, a deep abiding grief. A melancholy feeling layered with personal loss and planetary decay, endless wars, disappearing species and a climate of greed and intolerance pervaded even moments of light-hearted joy. Eleven-headed Kannon reminded me how far I had yet to travel. Would my pilgrimage bring me a step higher on that metaphorical ladder? Too often, it seemed, I felt hurled around in the sea of *samsara* trying to catch a glimpse of that magic ship on the horizon before I drowned. Tossed between hope and despair, optimism and pessimism, faith and doubt, I proceeded forward into the unknown, toward the only place that made sense: the next pilgrimage temple.

Chapter 17

I did not know
Imakumano had existed
Since ancient times—
Kannon's vow
Is ever renewed

Imakumano Kannonji – Temple 15

Bokefuji Kannon

As we crossed over the vermillion bridge and symbolically left the ordinary world to partake in the sacred atmosphere of Kannonji, I felt gratitude for the half dozen kind souls who had helped us find the right temple. Since we had let ourselves be carried away by a wave of sightseers out to enjoy the fall colors and beautiful sunny day in Kyoto, we had temporarily lost our way. But the spirit of the Kannon pilgrimage would not have it. Diverted through a neighborhood pottery festival, we eventually got directed to the Sennyuji Buddhist complex, a 57-acre "tranquil oasis" on the fringe of bustling Kyoto. Linked to Seigantoji and the Kumano Primeval Forest through the Shinto deity Kumano Gongen, said to have appeared to Kobo Daishi in the form of an old man who gave him a small statue of Eleven-headed Kannon, Kobo Daishi requested Emperor Saga to build a temple at this site. Ten centuries later, Imakumano Kannonji, Temple 15, still stands ready to receive pilgrims, especially those seeking to escape the suffering of dementia and Alzheimer's.

Perhaps Kumano Gongen still manifested as an old man. At Kannonji we saw a well-dressed gentleman sitting on the bare ground at the side of the temple repeatedly brushing his pant leg—a sign of severe senile dementia. All alone, without caretaker, spouse, or friend, this thin and tiny, but dignified man, opened my heart with compassion for the elderly worldwide with this disease. I had, years earlier, provided flower arranging activities at adult family homes for those with dementia. Alzheimer residents exhibited mild to severe symptoms, from chanting the same word over and over, to rocking back and forth, to outbursts of anger and confusion, to quiet moments of not remembering anything of their former lives, marriages or careers. In our society, most people never see this hidden world of the elderly.

At Imakumano Kannonji a special Kannon has been established for those hoping to ward off this memory disease. Bokefuji Kannon, with her very own pilgrimage route of ten temples, compassionately looks down upon an elderly man and woman who sit like helpless children at her feet. Since pilgrimage in Japan, as elsewhere, has become a commercial enterprise, it is no surprise that religious marketers have come up with the Bokefuji statue and pilgrim tour in a country with an aging population. It is easy to fall into cynicism when reading or hearing about, what could be interpreted as, religious exploitation. But for those with dementia, or those who know of a parent, friend or relative with dementia, the ability to connect with a form known for her compassionate nature, is a great comfort. She links us with, and elicits our own compassion, and in this sense, no matter who has designed this modern religious icon—even if for monetary gain—the real purpose, of bringing us closer to our innate Buddha-nature, is fulfilled.

A prayer from the Bokefuji pilgrimage leaflet thus states:

Living joy,
Life that gives us life,
To the Kannon-sama of the ten temples,
Let us pray for the prevention of senility.

Collecting another handful of maple leaves—golden ones this time—we proceeded to the hondo and the nokyocho office where the priest gave us a Kannon prayer card as a gift. He didn't say a word, just handed them over as, I presumed, an acknowledgement of our effort at having come this far on the pilgrimage. His quiet gesture of goodwill, one of many encountered on our journey, left an indelible imprint on our mind stream.

After our pilgrim rituals, we had tea and sweets at the temple, all part of the general festivities of the neighborhood on a beautiful autumn day in Kyoto. Then we visited the 33 Kannon shrines built into the hillside behind the hondo, a mini-pilgrimage that looked a bit neglected. The once colorful clothes and aprons that sometimes adorn deities looked tattered, faded and caked with dust. No fresh flower offerings adorned the shrines. No one walked the path.

Some people in Japan thought of religious pilgrimage as a tired, old-fashioned concept only suitable for superstitious country folk—and indeed many cultural studies point to the decline of institutional Buddhism in the Land of the Rising Sun. After all, Kannon pilgrims had been making their way around the Kansai for over one thousand years. What could possibly be fresh and modern about that? Even so, whether for religious/ spiritual development, adventurous tourist outings, celebrations of seasonal color, or ways to reconnect with traditional Japanese culture, pilgrimages had gained popularity in recent years. I surmised then that the mini-pilgrimage behind the main hall simply didn't offer the modern pilgrim any good photo ops or fall color.

Before long, I too found the most stunning scene and clicked away under bright sunny skies imprinted with red maples and vermillion pagodas. I too was happy to celebrate natural beauty rather than focus on human suffering I felt powerless to alleviate. Like everyone else, I wanted to savor the beauty of the day, the autumn colors, the warmth of the sun, a moment of tea with my sister... My time would come soon enough.

Chapter 18

The entreaties made on our visit
Are enfolded by Fujidera,
Just as we see a purple cloud
Cradled in the wisteria flowers

Fujidera – Temple 5

The Heart Sutra under Purple Clouds

The "purple cloud" in Fujidera's goeika has a double meaning: on the surface it refers to the vast canopy of wisteria that covers the temple complex in May, but on a metaphorical level it symbolizes Kannon herself directing wandering ascetics to the sites of sacred places—"a purple cloud hovering over…". Fill in the blank to complete the founding temple story line in many ancient legends.

Given that we were traveling the pilgrimage route in November, I had to imagine the splendor of Fujidera's "wisteria purple cloud," not to mention the temple's principal image, Senju or Thousand-armed Kannon only displayed on the 18th of each month—a week after we arrived. Even so, the beauty and tranquility of this neighborhood temple found at the end of a shopping arcade in a suburb of Osaka, pleasantly surprised me with its long history and calm atmosphere.

After a two-hour train ride through the never ending metropolis of the Kansai region, one appreciates even more the quiet serenity of ancient temples tucked into every little neighborhood throughout Japan. Appreciation also rises when you discover that a temple like Fujidera—destroyed countless times by war, including World War II when it was completely wiped out—is always rebuilt; and that the Senju Kannon, carved in 725, survived.

War being what it is, with its descent into the hell of hatred and violence, I found it extraordinary that after the Battle of Fujidera in the 14th century, the winning side of several hundred soldiers copied the Heart Sutra 600 times each and offered them to the temple. Even today, the practice of copying the Heart Sutra as an offering to the temple—in essence to the Buddha—is a common pilgrim practice.

The Heart Sutra, probably the most popular and well known of Mahayana Buddhist sutras, is still recited every day in Buddhist monasteries and dharma centers around the world. A modern interpretation of this venerable teaching, whose original title is "The Sutra of the Heart of the Glorious Lady Prajanaparamita," can be found in Mitra Karl Brunnhölzl's book *The Heart Attack Sutra*, the title implying that, like several of Buddha's followers, we might suffer sudden coronary arrest if we truly understood the real and profound truth revealed in this sutra.

Brunnhölzl goes on to explain that the Heart Sutra negates everything we know; it negates all that we cherish and believe to be real and substantial, including the Mahayana path of Buddhism. Deities, practices, rituals... even Kannon, are all "empty," in essence dream like, non-substantial, non-findable.

I have chanted the Heart Sutra many times, in English and Japanese, at Zen, Chan and Tibetan Buddhist temples, and each time I've tried to make sense of essentially nonsensical words meant to scramble conceptual framework and boot one out of ordinary thinking. After twenty years' exposure to this ancient sutra maybe I've had a tiny glimpse into its meaning, but nothing sudden or shocking enough to generate a heart attack. Perhaps I should appreciate the wisdom inherent in the gradual process of awakening rather than lament that I haven't yet experienced that sudden burst of enlightenment.

The practice of copying the Heart Sutra first came into my realm of experience at Saiho-ji or Kokedera (Moss Temple) in Kyoto, a garden that requires a permit through advance application. Before touring the garden, every visitor (about 70 people on the day of our scheduled time) sits at a low writing table on top of a tatami mat and copies the Heart Sutra—270 kanji characters. I laid my piece of translucent "rice" paper over the kanji template, and with sumi ink and a calligraphy brush, spent the next forty minutes silently and delicately tracing the characters with my brush. When finished, I signed my name with the date and gave it to the temple steward. Presumably, my mind had achieved the calm state needed to appreciate the subtleties of the 120 varieties of moss displayed throughout the garden.

With that one experience in my memory banks, I imagined that after completing 600 copies—especially if I had previously been engaged in battle and killed other human beings—I might feel somewhat cleansed and purified of negativity and bad karma. Additionally, I would have immersed myself in the quintessential teaching of the ultimate nature of reality and the truth of existence. Such is the essence of the Heart Sutra; it breaks down all of our false notions of reality, jumbles them up and leaves us wondering what is at the heart of being human, of being alive.

The Heart Sutra is so popular and widespread in Japan that students who study ikebana at the Saga Goryu School's Headquarters at Daikakuji (my own ikebana school) chant this sutra, along with the head priest, before receiving instructions. Most, if not all, Japanese have been familiar with this ancient and holy sutra since childhood, a teaching that says "form is empty and emptiness is form," a teaching that alludes to the nature of the enlightened mind and the lack of any substantial inherent existence of ourselves and the objects around us. Although the language of the Heart Sutra might appear to be esoteric or difficult to understand, nonetheless the power of the words, both spoken and written, are said to create their own effect whether you understand them or not. The Heart Sutra then has permeated the Japanese culture for over 1,000 years, and whether Japanese consider themselves Buddhist or secular modernists, the wisdom of the Heart Sutra would seem to live on in their DNA.

As I reflected on this and the ramifications of military personnel copying the Heart Sutra at Fujidera, the rain that day, rather than wisteria petals, kept pouring down. But even with wet feet and dripping umbrellas, I appreciated the dharma revealed. The story pointed to, not only the importance of the Heart Sutra, but the power inherent in recitation of holy prayers and teachings, and my own long neglect of chant—once a large part of my daily practice. The soldiers at Fujidera left an inspiring legacy that even in the 21st century served to inspire this Buddhist practitioner. Intent on renewing my practice of reciting and studying the Heart Sutra, and inspired to copy those 271 kanji characters over and over once I got home, I purchased a template of the Japanese version of the Heart Sutra. Before my return trip, I planned to copy at least one sutra for each temple on our pilgrimage, and offer the merit of the practice to a conflict brewing in some part of the world. Intention coupled with the ritual of copying a sacred document, promised to leave positive imprints in the collective unconscious, or "The Field," as Lynne McTaggart calls the unseen world that connects us all.

In the meantime, we absorbed all that Fujidera had to offer, including two humorous flat wooden replicas of a pilgrim and a wandering priest with cut-outs for the face of the modern day pilgrim. Gwen couldn't resist. She stood behind the pilgrim and peered out from under the brim of the traditional conical hat. With camera in one hand and umbrella in the other, I managed to capture her smiling irreverent face—even pilgrims should laugh at themselves now and then. Shortly after, the rain stopped and the sun came out. We took a more leisurely stroll under the wisteria trellis to view the mini-pilgrimage of 33 Kannon manifestations.

Unlike the one at Imakumano Kannonji, Fujidera's mini-pilgrimage looked well tended with tidy grounds and fresh flowers arranged in built-in flower vases. Every month the temple hosts a mini-market place with fresh produce and other goods, so the temple takes pride in providing a beautiful sanctuary for harried city dwellers.

For a small temple complex, Fujidera had several other noteworthy points of interest. The statue of *Sonshinryu* Kannon or "Kannon Riding on the Precious Heart Dragon," a bronze sculpture with Kannon's flowing robes intertwined with the dragon's writhing body, expressed the union of male and female, wisdom and compassion, calm serenity and divine wrathfulness. To a person born under the sign of the dragon now on pilgrimage in the Year of the Dragon, an icon of the dragon and Kannon together resonated with my personal journey. Perhaps my own masculine and feminine sides, my own wisdom and compassion, would become more wholly integrated on this pilgrimage. Would I gain more clarity in discerning when to be passive and when to be active in tackling life's challenges?

Fujidera presented powerful symbols to contemplate and deepen one's understanding of the Buddhist way, but its long history of being subjected to battle and wars brought my prayers around to those still caught in the tragedy of violent conflict throughout the world. In my own country, which at the time had entered its eleventh year fighting terrorists in Afghanistan, and its ninth year of fighting in Iraq, war had become a perpetual story with no end in sight.

The Institute for Economics and Peace tracks worldwide conflict and issues a Global Peace Index (GPI). They state that the world has been growing less peaceful over the last decade, and that in 2014 only 11 countries worldwide remained free of conflict. Japan is one of those 11, ranking #9 out of 162 countries with the U.S. ranking #103.

The world, still waiting for the purple cloud of sacred vision to direct us to the mountain of holy peace, still waiting for wisdom and compassion to guide our actions, stands at a precipice. Will we self-destruct? When so many in power still think that violent action is a path to peace and happiness, we can only shudder in disbelief.

At Fujidera, the temple that survived and continues to offer respite despite centuries of past conflict, pilgrims come to stand under the glory of that ephemeral purple, still praying—as millions do every day, at mosques, synagogues, cathedrals, temples and other sacred places—for that elusive of states: world peace.

Chapter 19

The source of this spring
Where does it begin?
At Iwamadera
The waves crash upon the shore
In the sound of wind in the pines

Iwamadera – Temple 12

Raven and the Sacred Trees

Once we surrendered to taxi transportation from Ishiyamadera to Iwamadera rather than public transportation, we soon found ourselves flying through narrow one-way streets and turning onto an even narrower mountain road that rose steadily up and around several dizzying switch-backs. In less than twenty minutes, our taxi landed in the parking lot of Temple 12— also known as Shoboji or True Dharma Temple—which left us wondering why reaching this place had once seemed so daunting.

I took a deep breath of fresh mountain air and felt a pang of expectation. What would be revealed at this minor temple not on any tourist circuit? A whole world of possibility, revelation and surprise awaited.

The driveway, lined with stone lanterns, brought us to our first stop: a scenic overlook to view the layers of mountains ever present in the Kansai region. Always another layer of mountains, the geographical tiers mirrored the cultural ones of symbol, legend, hidden meaning and subtle nuance.

Across from the view, a statue of Bokefuji Kannon, the bodhisattva who comforts those with dementia and Alzheimer's brought us back to memories of Imagumano Kannonji where we both mistook the two human figures at Kannon's feet to be children—similar to the many depictions of Jizo Bodhisattva who protects babies and youth. But now, on closer examination, the figures, clearly elders in the *posture* of children, sought with their meek gestures Kannon's compassion. Remembering the elderly man with dementia sitting on the ground at Kannonji, and the many parents of friends who have fallen under dementia's cruel tyranny, we stopped to make prayers. Bokefuji Kannon brought forth the gravity of all that we had yet to encounter in our own aging process. No longer young enough to blissfully ignore life's possibilities, or to pretend that such things as forgetting ones own identity couldn't happen to us, we solemnly and silently headed toward the entrance gate, and our second important icon.

At all Buddhist temples in Japan, two wrathful guardian statues—*Nio* in Japanese, or Vajrapani in the Mahayana pantheon—stand on either side of the front gate. They symbolically protect the temple and all that is contained within by frightening away anything that might violate the values, beliefs, and teachings of Buddhism. The guardian on the right, with mouth open, represents birth; the guardian on the left, with mouth closed, represents death. The space between them represents The Absolute, or all that is contained between birth and death. At Iwamadera, the Nio, a distinctive ebony and shiny as lacquer, enhanced their ferocious, don't-mess-with-me muscular stance. If they were meant to instill fear, they did. Somehow, in a remote enclave such as Iwamadera, known for Shugendo—a Buddhist sect that uses austere mountain practices to achieve higher states of consciousness—the ebony Nio lent to the serious and fearsome atmosphere of this place.

But if the Nio, in their body-builder countenance, represented the quintessential power of wrathful maleness, the next marvel represented the opposite. Inside the temple compound the autumn wonder of a golden ginkgo tree shimmered under the November sun like a queen at a coronation.

The ginkgo tree, surrounded by a special plaited rope or

shimenawa that indicated the presence of kami, or a nature deity, had the largest trunk of any ginkgo I'd ever encountered in Japan. Its very presence induced awe and respect, much like a giant redwood, cedar or oak—trees that inspire with their grandeur. The ginkgo can live up to 1,500 years, which made this particular specimen well beyond several centuries. We stood under its falling gold leaves and extolled its beauty while searching the ground for perfect leaf specimens—leaves shaped like Japanese fans, and treasured for their unique beauty.

The Japanese regard the gingko as the bearer of hope, longevity, resilience and peace, due to the fact that four ginkgos survived the atomic bombing of Hiroshima, and still live to this day. The Urasenke Tea School that espouses, "peace in a bowl of tea," utilizes the gingko leaf as their emblem. The design can be found everywhere in Japan, from ceramics to textiles to confections; it has been immortalized throughout the centuries in dozens of Japanese poems and haiku. Thus gingko leaves in Japan have reached near talismanic levels.

Behind the gingko, next to the temple garden, a tranquil pond, billed as "the place" where Basho, the famous haiku poet of the 17th century, observed a frog jumping and wrote, "Old pond/frog jumps into/the sound of water," offers quiet contemplation. The haiku, considered a classic example of a short poem that captures the moment of awakening, has elicited many commentaries throughout the centuries. Basho—a student of Zen, and a Kannon devotee—journeyed to this mountain temple in 1687 for a retreat. Although another pond near Tokyo also claims to be the location of Basho's "old pond" haiku inspiration, Iwamadera offered the potential for an "enlightenment" experience. The quiet remoteness of this mountainside gave the temple complex an atmosphere conducive to spiritual insight.

Very few pilgrims make the effort to visit Temple 12. In fact our inquiry at the Kyoto Tourist Center perplexed the woman behind the counter. "Why do you want to go there?" she asked.

"It's too far." Her tone implied that Iwamadera had nothing special to make it worth the effort.

After basking in the aura of the ginkgo tree and Basho's frog pond, we wandered past the main temple and down a pathway that led to a miniature pilgrimage of thirty-three Kannon shrines. Here the sound of a raven and its incessant cawing began to follow us everywhere. The raven cawed as we walked from shrine to shrine; it cawed when we went out to view the other sacred tree, a giant katsura or Japanese Judas tree said to be over 1,000 years old; it cawed when we went over to the wild area to view the vast arching trunks and branches of the katsura and to take in the tiny house built for the kami that protected this sacred tree; it cawed while we read the founding legend, about the eighth-century priest who saw a purple cloud hovering near the present site of the katsura tree and heard the voice of Kannon reciting sacred praises; and it cawed when we strolled along the pathway leading back to the temple. The raven kept cawing, frantically at times, as if trying to get and keep our attention. Raven seemed to be saying, "Look! Don't you see?"

I wondered what message or insight Iwamadera would reveal. What aspect of Buddha's teaching would Kannon direct her light? I had already encountered and written about Bokefuji Kannon. Should I say more about the special pilgrimage that she now resides over? Would the striking black Nio at the front gate impart some unique wisdom? Surely reams could be written about dharma protectors and guardians of the dharma. What about the mysterious rites of Shugendo practitioners who believe that nature provides a portal to awakening? No doubt there were many stories to be revealed about the lives of these mountain ascetics who lived and practiced on Mt. Iwama. But that would be highlighted in the chapter on Kami Daigoji, Temple 11. And what about the "sacred" well at this temple, said to be dug by the hands of a thunder god? What mysteries lay hidden inside this ancient myth?

But Raven persisted. And later, I would hear it say, "The trees. Don't forget the trees. The place where I live." I would think about trees—sacred trees, ordinary trees, ordinary trees as sacred—throughout the rest of the trip. Iwamadera had three stunning sacred trees containing centuries of history and legend. Was Kannon, through the voice of Raven, sending a message?

Concerned about keeping our taxi driver waiting too long, we reluctantly made ready to leave. After traveling to eighteen of the thirty-three Kannon temples, we began to accept that time never allowed us to absorb all that each temple contained, or the depth of meaning in each statue, pond, tree, pagoda, rock.... So too Iwamadera. On our short visit we merely discovered the first layer of possibility, much like the subtle meaning of an impressionistic poem.

As the afternoon sun moved toward the far side of the mountain, and thoughts of our long journey back to Kyoto nagged at us, we couldn't linger any longer. With our temple books stamped and a few choice ginkgo leaves tucked into our purses, we left Iwamadera with the sound of Raven cawing and the feeling that something mysterious, something we couldn't quite name, had transpired at this simple mountain temple.

All through the rest of the trip, Raven's voice haunted me. I would sit down to write in the early morning hours and hear the sound of Raven, cawing his head off. The sacred trees of Iwamadera prompted me to research trees: trees in peril, ancient forests threatened with annihilation, old growth wonders on "death row." Deforestation, or the cutting down of forests to create land for non-forest use has been escalating out of control over the last 50 years. The first statistic that hit with the thud of finality: "Since 1947, half of the earth's mature tropical forests have been destroyed." We were annihilating the very entities that gave us life: the oxygen that we breathe.

But what could I do about all the atrocities committed against trees and forests? My own ancestors had already logged most of the primeval forests in Europe and North America to make way for grazing and farmland. Now, in the 21st century, the tropical rainforests, once completely untouched wilderness, are meeting the same tragic fate.

The great tree guru of our generation, Dr. Wangari Maathai, the woman who single-handedly mobilized ordinary people around the globe to plant a billion trees, had touted the Japanese adage *"mottainai,"* which roughly means "waste nothing," a Buddhist principle of respecting all objects, both human made and those from nature. The Buddha recognized that everything we have or own requires natural resources and human labor; that a great expenditure of time and energy went into creating objects for our everyday use and pleasure. We shouldn't take objects for granted, but remember where they came from. How many trees had to perish for, say, a ream of paper to write a book, or build a writing desk? Was I honoring each piece of paper in my daily life? Were my words worthy of the paper I used? Raven inspired a more mindful assessment of the time, energy, labor and natural resources that went into making the "things" I took for granted. He/she made me pause to remember the Buddhist precept "no killing," and "do no harm."

Generally, I related to this precept by not eating meat, not killing insects (when I could avoid it), not "killing" someone's enthusiasm or spirit by being negative, not putting anything into the environment that would harm it or others. But viewing trees as sacred, I had to further acknowledge the living, breathing planet that contained our lives. Trees, responsible for the very air that we breathed, all had an element of the sacred. Without trees we would become extinct, and yet we were annihilating most of the earth's rainforests in favor of pasture land for livestock.

Dr. Wangari Maathai, the great bodhisattva of trees, received the Right Livelihood Award for her work to preserve and plant trees. Under Buddha's Noble Eightfold Path, "Right Livelihood" is number five. I speculated that the other seven—

Right View, Intention, Speech, Action, Effort, Mindfulness and Concentration—had all been employed by Dr. Maathai in her campaign to stop deforestation.

Dr. Maathai stressed that like the Japanese we should go beyond the 3Rs—Re-use, Recycle, Reduce—and add Respect and Gratitude. She said, "...the planting of trees is the planting of ideas. By starting with the simple step of digging a hole and planting a tree, we plant hope for ourselves and for future generations."

Raven extolled the virtues of the late Dr. Wangari Maathai; its black feathery head moving into a great cosmic caw of acknowledgement. Iwamadera, "The Source of this spring [of spiritual awakening] where waves crash upon the shore, in the sound of wind in the pines," a wind blowing through the world's forests beseeching us to hear its prayer: Gratitude and Respect.

Through "skillful means," Raven spoke of the blessed qualities of all trees, all forests, and the symbiotic relationship between us. This mythic bird—a harbinger of cosmic messages in Native lore and called upon by shamans for clarity and insight—left its imprint along with the goeika's lament, a poem-prayer extolling the virtues of Iwamadera. This ancient chant carried forth into our own hearts and minds like the wind now blowing from Iwama Mountain, a wind blowing inspiration and blessings all the way across the Pacific.

Thousand-armed Kannon at Iwamadera, through her many compassionate arms and eyes, represents protection and guidance from all evils, including natural disasters. Deforestation and the disaster of climate change *is* our 21st-century "evil." Raven seemed to be saying, "Wake up! Wake up to the sacred nature of trees! Before it's too late."

Chapter 20

Even with a heavy karma
Your suffering may be relieved
If you offer prayers
At the Junteido
There is hope

Kami Daigoji – Temple 11

Women in the Forbidden Zone

The word "daigo" in Sanskrit roughly means "spiritual bliss," but historically, whether you experienced rapture on Mt. Daigo or not depended on your gender: most females (except for a handful of aristocrats) were banned from this mountain for over 1,300 years. These days, only Mt. Sanjo in the Yoshino-Kumano National Park region still bans women (although feminists have been known to breach the restriction). Even so, once we began our trek to Upper Daigoji I felt that perhaps women still weren't entirely welcome on this mountain. The male hikers seemed a bit unfriendly, odd on a hike in Japan where everyone greets each other with "*Ohayo gozaimasu!*" (Good morning!) or "*Konnichiwa!*" (Good afternoon!). None of our guide books or web information mentioned the rather frosty attitude of men, and it was the last thing on our radar screen. Rather, the strenuous nature of the hike, the weather, and our health concerns occupied our thoughts instead.

The trek to the top of Mt. Daigo is only 1.8 miles, but with an elevation gain of nearly 1,500 feet the ascent promised to be steady and steep. Our guidebook described it thus: "Unless you're a regular mountain hiker, the path to Kami Daigoji is nothing less than a draining journey, requiring concentration and strength in equal." Consequently, we thought it best to time our hike with favorable weather conditions. Already late November, good weather became less and less predictable. Coupled with my procrastination when it came to anything worrisome or frightening, and my previous heart condition, the thought of hiking to Upper Daigo Temple gave me serious pause. Five years ago, I had come close to having a heart attack due to a semi-blocked artery. Two stents later, and thirty-five pounds lighter, I felt healthy and fit, but never confident whether another blocked artery would sneak up on me. Visions of being a medical emergency at the top of a mountain with my poor sister trying to cope with the situation in her rudimentary Japanese plagued my thoughts. Although dying on pilgrimage had a history of auspiciousness, I didn't relish the idea.

Gwen had her own fears: a painful ankle injury that flared up occasionally and a habit of tripping. Her nightmare looked like pitching headfirst down a long flight of stone stairs and landing at the bottom with severe concussion. Neither of us shared these worries until later.

Needless to say, we left Kami Daigoji to the end of our trip, partly because of our fears, and partly because we kept waiting for guaranteed good weather. Our chosen day promised to be sunny and mild, and so, fortified with several deep breaths, drinking water and lunch, we headed out.

A day hike from Kyoto, Mt. Daigo and the Shingon-Daigo Buddhist temple complex is an ancient pilgrimage site and training ground for present day *yamabushi:* mountain ascetics who practice Shugendo (The Way of Acquiring Spiritual Power). Through meditation, chanting and severe physical austerities (such as sitting under icy waterfalls or being suspended over high cliffs), practitioners strive to connect with nature in order to open a pathway or portal to higher consciousness. Shugendo, banned as a superstitious practice during the Meiji Period when the government forcibly separated Shinto and Buddhism, became reinstated in 1946. Today this quasi-Buddhist sect's philosophy includes a kind of eco-environmentalism that advocates re-connecting with nature, protecting the environment, eating vegetarian food, growing your own organic garden and partaking in community and family life as a healthy, balanced and saner way to live. Both men and women—known as Shugenja—practice the religion, although some of the practices remain gender restricted.

Shugenja consider mountains to be sacred mother figures: protective, nurturing, life-giving. In this regard it is no surprise that Daigoji would have *Juntei* Kannon (Mother Kannon, and the only one on the Saigoku pilgrimage) as its representative principle image—but nonetheless ironic that it also had a history of not allowing women to the top of the mountain. Tragically, in 2008, Kami Daigoji lost its Mother Kannon temple and sacred icons in a devastating fire. I sensed that, psychologically, the temple community had yet to recover. Per the goeika, prayers could no longer be offered at the Junteido to relieve one's "heavy karma." Had "hope" also been lost? Even as late as 2012, the Daigoji website stated that the upper temple complex remained closed due to reconstruction, even though we found that not to be true. The "closure" felt more like a statement of mourning, or perhaps psychic shock that nature had destroyed their beloved sanctuary that enshrined all the symbols of Divine Mother worship.

History and gender issues aside, it is advisable to hike to the top of Daigoji on a day when the forecast promises clement weather, unless you find descending steep rocky steps made slippery by rain and wet leaves thrilling. In fall (roughly mid-November) one reaps the added benefit of stunning autumn foliage, particularly at Lower Daigo Temple, a designated UNESCO World Cultural Heritage Site famous for a thousand-year-old five-storied pagoda. In spring (roughly mid-April) Daigoji promises to dazzle with Japan's other seasonal obsession: cherry blossoms—made famous here by Shogun Hideyoshi's extravagant cherry blossom parties, commemorated every year on the second Sunday of April when one thousand cherry trees transform into "pink clouds."

Before ascending the mountain, we toured the Lower Daigo Temple complex, and discovered that the temple stewards now stamped the pilgrim's book in the lower hondo. This meant that the arduous climb to Upper Daigo, no longer technically necessary for the "you were here" stamp, gave the cowardly part of me a perfect opportunity to back out. If my sister had indicated the least hesitation and allowed me an easy escape, I would still be wondering how we would have faired on that mountain, and berating myself for being too chicken to find out. Instead, I had an opportunity to practice the Paramitas of Effort and Resolve.

Resolved or not, in case something *did* happen to me, I wanted my stamp before the climb. We found the temple scribe, got our books stamped, and tried to ask about prayer cards depicting this temple's unique Juntei Kannon. He either didn't understand our Japanese or didn't want to. The cards, always prevalent at other pilgrimage temples, didn't appear to exist at Daigoji — one of many absences that felt troubling.

Undaunted, we toured the grounds and pond around the Bentendo hall, a small shrine dedicated to the popular Benzaiten, the beloved muse of anyone engaged in an artistic discipline. Again it struck me that a temple that had forbidden women to the upper regions of its sacred mountain for centuries, worshipped two very prominent female deities: Mother Kannon and Benzaiten — the feminine embraced but not the female embodiment?

For the time being I put that thought aside to take in the stunning red maples and gold gingko's surrounding the pond, and the vermillion lacquered bridge that transported visitors to the goddesses' shrine. The pond reflected blue sky, fall leaves and that stunning bridge. White swans seemingly swam through the vast sky. This "Pure Land" scene erased any irksome, negative thoughts in favor of lightness and joy. Nature and the aesthetic pleasures of Japanese gardens tended to do that.

Further along, and right before the entrance to Upper Daigoji, we stopped to dedicate the merit of our trek to all suffering beings, a tradition honored by pouring water over the heads of the five noteworthy figures bearing witness to the pilgrim's intent: Fudo Myo-o (the Light King and central figure of Shugendo), Shobo Rigen Daishi (founder of Daigo Temple), Maitreya (the future Buddha), En no Gyoja (founder of Shugendo) and Jizo Bodhisattva (protector of women, children and travelers). I poured ladle after ladle of water over all five heads, and made special prayers for a safe journey and a friend suffering from depression.

Having solidified my vow to make it to the top on behalf of others, we proceeded past the *Nyonin-do*, or "Women's Temple" the traditional stopping point for females before the law changed in 1872 eliminating gender bias on most of Japan's sacred mountains. But first we had to pay another fee (presumably for climbing the mountain), and only then were we allowed through the turnstile that led to Upper Daigoji.

Once we started our climb and began encountering other hikers, we experienced the difference in attitude between men and women. The men seemed a bit hesitant or guarded, whereas the women (and we encountered several) smiled, greeted us and often stopped to chat in English. Hmm! The banning or not banning of women from sacred mountains has been, and still is controversial. Still, all the more reason for women to hike this mountain and for men to show their support in eradicating sexual discrimination—still justified under the guise of "gender segregation."

Historically, women have had to struggle for equality in every major world religion, including Buddhism, a religion that prides itself on the eradication of ignorance. Even Buddha

Shakyamuni, the awakened master who gave birth to Buddhism, initially refused to allow women to ordain. When questioned by his close disciple Ananda on whether women were capable of attaining enlightenment, the Buddha answered in the affirmative, but still refused to allow them to become disciples. Ananda persisted, arguing that women should be allowed to take vows and follow in the footsteps of his master. Five years after Buddha's awakening, he finally acquiesced and ordained the first woman, his stepmother and aunt, Mahapajapati, but only after she had made three requests, cut off her hair, donned the saffron robes and followed Buddha wherever he traveled. Even so, some traditional Buddhists believe that women are unable to attain enlightenment in a female form. And in centuries past, women who wanted to join monasteries mutilated their faces so as not to be a distraction to monks. They also had to accept eight rules that established their irrefutable inferiority to monks no matter their seniority or spiritual attainments. Monks could criticize and revile a nun, but a nun was forbidden to do the same to a monk.

* * *

Our climb began up the wide earthen steps terraced into the mountain with wood beams and a lot of hard work. I marveled at the engineering and manual labor that went into creating the hundreds of stone stairs that switch-backed up these mountains. The story of this remarkable feat has most probably been lost to the greater legends of the founding of this temple site — a vision by the priest Shobo in 874 of a five-colored cloud hovering over the mountain top. The stone stairs, worn smooth as a counter top by thousands of worshippers trekking the Kannon route, transported us too into the mystical atmosphere of the once thriving complex of 200 temples. Now, this Shingon-Daigo Buddhist community has been reduced to a handful of structures made smaller still after the fire.

With gratitude to the many unknown hands who contributed such an aesthetically pleasing staircase, we huffed and puffed our way up to the first rest stop—a sacred waterfall guarded by a Shinto kami, or nature deity, and dedicated to Fudo Myo-o, the Light King: dispeller of ignorance, who fearsomely cuts through human delusions with his wisdom sword. Here we stopped for a snack in the covered alcove, and reflected on being 21st-century females who could now travel to sacred places once off limits to women. We could freely practice Buddhism, ordain, teach, attain the highest states in a female form—nothing remained off limits. Only the history of women being repressed and oppressed remained as memories or imprints that perhaps still lived in our DNA. How could these dark shadows be expunged? The lingering anger eradicated? Perhaps by making it to the top of Mt. Daigo some small amount of restitution would be granted.

Fortified with food and committed to reaching the summit, we moved on, confident that our sunny autumn day would continue well into the afternoon. Others had presumed the same we suspected, as we passed several hikers who had forgone coats and day packs. One man wore a business suit; his young female companion sported fashionable high-heeled boots. Shortly after our urban "escapees," we passed another *cho* or meter marker, but by now we'd lost count and relied instead on simply looking ahead for the crest. About two-thirds of the way we came to a large stone turtle carrying a stone tablet with engraved print (presumably a sutra of some kind). The bell beside the turtle begged to be struck three times to acknowledge the three jewels of Buddhism, and to encourage others making the ascent. I rang the bell as a reminder to take refuge in Buddha, Dharma and Sangha rather than the material world. Given the sunny day, beautiful mountain scenery, and stunning fall leaves, the illusory dreamlike world of the hike itself threatened to undermine our bodhisattva intention to offer merit for all suffering beings—

particularly women— to fulfill our pilgrim's vow, and polish those Perfections.

With each bend along the trail promising to be the last, we sympathized with others coming up behind, who, like us, must also be experiencing the mirage-like illusion of the trail's end. Sensing again and again that the top of the mountain must surely be in reach, we quickened our pace, only stopping periodically to examine the red and gold maple leaves lying on the ground.

A record year for fall colors, we couldn't resist looking for perfect specimens to press in our travel book. Gwen observed the metaphor of our actions: seeking perfection and being disappointed when one never finds it. I said that I rather liked some of the flaws in the leaves—rotted spots, a blotch of odd coloring, an insect hole—but she detected my half-truth, noting all the times I had exclaimed, "Ah, look at this one," in reference to a near flawless leaf. When she stopped again to pick up a perfect leaf, I responded that we'd never make it to the top if we stopped to look at all the leaves.

Lured forward by the promise of sighting the plateau around the next turn—and being fooled one more time—when we finally *did* reach the first temple building—now closed with the look of having been abandoned for years—I proclaimed that we had come far enough. But Gwen, forever prodding me to go beyond my limitations and determined to follow the trail to the very end, urged us onward only to find the trail going down instead of up.

The down part didn't last long before we were confronted with one more set of steep stairs that led to what appeared to be the final temple: the *Godai-do*. Inside this dark cavernous hall, shiny glass eyes and blackened features of the five Kings of Light, with Fudo Myo-o at the center, stared back at us. The Myo-o Kings, originally adopted from Hinduism and incorporated into esoteric Buddhism, appear as wrathful deities protecting Buddhist doctrine. The images evoked esoteric practices of a powerful tantric nature and indeed related to the yamabushi practitioners of Shugendo. We stopped to make offerings of incense and lighted candles. A statue of Shugendo founder En no Gyoja stood outside the Godai-do in front of a mandala-like cement fire pit used in the Goma Fire Ceremony, a purification rite.

The Goma Ceremony, a powerful cleansing or purifying ritual in Shingon Buddhism, involves rapid chanting and drum beating during which the head priest tosses prayers and petitions written on wooden sticks into a blazing fire symbolizing the mouth of heaven, or Buddha's wisdom. The crackling flames and vigorous chanting induce a trancelike state where one feels purged of negativity; disquieting thoughts are calmed, desires are subdued; good fortune is bestowed. The one I attended years ago left a strong impression and brought back memories of the power of consecrated fire to psychologically "wash" the mind of impurities. I thought again of the word "daigo" or "bliss" also translated as "ambrosia," a metaphor for the sustenance given to Buddha before his final awakening. Perhaps one could begin to get a taste for spiritual bliss in the throws of a fire purification ceremony on top of Mt. Daigo.

As we sat down on a wooden bench near the fire pit to finish the rest of our lunch, the rather foreboding atmosphere on this mountain top began to seep in. With the weathered abandoned temple buildings, fierce looking statues with glinting eyes and the empty ground where the *Juntei-do* had been struck by lightening, Kami Daigoji possessed a special power not to be taken lightly.

The wind rose up from below and rustled the trees. "The weather's changing," I said, noting fear at the thought of being caught up here in a sudden rainstorm. I worried about maneuvering steep stone stairs made slick from hard driving rain so typical this time of year. "We should get going."

Without another word, we finished our lunch, packed up our

gear and took off. But as we reached the path leading back down the mountain, we noticed that it continued up and around the bend. Neither of us saw that path on the way up—odd since it was quite obvious.

Perplexed at our oversight, but determined not to be defeated by fear or worry, we pressed on to the *Nyorin-do*, or "Omnipotent Kannon Temple," and the most spectacular view of the surrounding mountains. In the distance, almost like a dreamscape, we could make out the skyscrapers of Osaka jutting up through hazy smog with the soft silhouette of the Japanese mountains all around. And yet even here the path continued, luring us on and upward to the final stop, the *Kaisan-do*, the temple dedicated to the founder of Kami Daigoji. From here there should have been an ancient path leading over the mountain to Iwamadera, another five- or six-hour hike. But we didn't see an alternative route other than the one going back the way we came, a loop that connected to the main trail. No other hikers appeared at this point, except for a man in his sixties who literally ran past us undaunted by the likelihood of tripping or falling over the rocks. We suspected he might be a Shugendo practitioner in training. Other than a quick glance, he didn't acknowledge us or us him. He disappeared as quickly as he had arrived.

Again the wind rose up, swirled up through the trees and sent leaves scattering. Were the forest kamis having fun with these two *gaijin*? The mountain exerting its power? Kami Daigoji didn't feel particularly welcoming, but not exactly hostile either; rather it manifested a poetically exciting atmosphere that sparked the imagination. Even the resident compound had an aura of mystery as the only sign of anyone living there came from billowing smoke rising above a stone wall. We didn't see anyone tending the fire or what they were burning, and joked later over a matcha latte that it could have been bodies for all we knew. "Women's bodies," Gwen added, and we laughed until tears rolled down our nose.

* * *

On the hike down, we held on to the guide rope to ensure that neither of us ended in a broken heap at the bottom. The descent took over an hour, and left our legs weak and wobbly, but our spirits high. Fears of heart attacks, falls, rain, slippery stones, unknown forces and all the other niggling nagging worries remained as so many shadows lurking in the background. We two women—who never would have had the opportunity in centuries past to visit the uppermost heights of this sacred mountain—left Daigoji with the thrill of completing the first 19 temples of our pilgrimage, a truly exhilarating finale.

* * *

Nine months after returning home, I tasted one of "the fruits" of confronting my fear of hiking to Upper Daigoji; I resumed my annual pilgrimage to Mt. Rainier to hike the flower meadows of Paradise—something I hadn't done since before my heart problems. In reaching for the compassion (and bliss) of Kannon on Kami Daigoji, an obstacle that kept me from enjoying one of my life's passions had resolutely dissolved.

Praises to Kannon for her "skillful means"!

Epilogue

The pilgrimage path, from the tops of mountains, to the valleys, and all urban and suburban enclaves, contained metaphors for our lives as we moved with the rising and falling of joy and grief, happiness and sadness, boredom and excitement and all the gray areas in between. The winds rose up and diminished, the leaves dropped from the trees and appeared as buds again in the spring—these truths, obvious and certain, gave stability to our lives. But everything else lay in the realm of the unknown, an uncertain journey with no predictable outcome.

The raven cawing frantically at Iwamadera, cried out to preserve the ancient trees; the loving arms of Bokefuji Kannon asked us to care for our elderly with compassion; the purple cloud of Fujidera reminded us that we have the power to create beauty in the same place that once held the ravages of war. The essence of each temple, each manifestation of Kannon called to our highest potential. What would we leave behind in the world? What would be worthy of our precious human lives?

Like the Japanese culture itself, our pilgrimage thus far had been one of contrasts. The busiest temple: Kiyomizudera, where one is literally carried through the temple along a human wave, contrasted with the least visited temple: Kami Daigoji, where we were the only two people at the top of the mountain. We remembered the warm hands of the old nun, and that of a chilly nokyo steward hidden behind a plastic *noren*; we gazed upon the one small, but beautiful Kannon on a distant mountain and craned our necks to take in the giant Kannon as big as a mountain; we saw hillsides covered with the red and yellow hues of autumn and ancient temples darkened over the centuries into every shade of brown and gray. The sweet feminine faces of Thousand-armed Kannon stood in contrast to the fierce warrior faces of Fudo Myo-o; the soft motherly kindness of

Bokefuji Kannon paled against the menacing stance of the Nio, or guardian deities; the lavish gardens with koi ponds, vermillion bridges and manicured moss juxtaposed with wild primeval forests and windy mountain tops exuding anything but "cultivated." Each temple possessed a distinctive character and feeling essence which reflected the 33 manifestations of Kannon. And yet I had to ask myself again and again, who or what is Kannon?

Conceptualized and depicted in various guises: Eleven-headed, Thousand-armed, motherly, masculine, feminine, cosmic, earthly—she seemed to be all things, yet not always a "she." And from a non-dual point of view, she could not be anymore "out there" than "in here." In other words she/he, a product of our imagination but as real as the warm touch of a human hand—numinous and earthly, ephemeral and concrete— could not be adequately described. Like theistic mystics in other religious traditions, the face of God, like Kannon, eluded definitions. She remained the essence of life, a creative force giving birth (thus feminine) to our reality and yet overlaid with a divine presence as luminous as the gold in a sacred ginkgo tree in autumn.

John Blofeld tries to pin down the nature of Kannon in his book *The Compassion of Kuan Yin*. Whether Chinese, Japanese or Tibetan, the Buddha of Compassion as described in the Lotus Sutra, the "Regarder of the Cries of the World Bodhisattva," is beyond "pinning down." She is at once a tangible real presence and ephemeral thought, a concept created to comfort, a source of enlightened power, an earthly mother and cosmic sunbeam. Blofeld tries and fails to define the definitive Kannon. In my attempt to wrap up a true picture of Kannon I resorted to the divination game using Kannon (or Guanyin) poems for an answer. Choosing a number with eyes closed, my finger landed on #5 "In the Darkness."

Dig deep into the earth where the spring water gushes
Through sheer pain and labor, seek to win through—
In a place like this, then, you come across a true friend
And seeing each other again (it's you!)
You both touch Heaven.

Part II

Preface

Between our first and second pilgrimage trips, Gwen and I exchanged health concerns. Whereas I had previously worried about my heart, and Gwen had worried about her foot, now Gwen worried about her heart and I worried about my foot.

About six months before our leave date, Gwen developed severe heart palpitations. After wearing a heart monitor for 48 hours, the cardiologist diagnosed her with High Frequency Premature Ventricular Contractions (PVCs). He recommended the full gamut of cardiac testing procedures (echocardiogram and nuclear stress test) to determine whether she had an artery blockage or valve problem. About the same time, I developed a painful bout of plantar fasciitis, which felt like someone had pounded a nail into the middle of my heel. Walking more than a couple of blocks made me limp with pain.

How would I tolerate all the walking, stair climbing and mountain hiking required on the pilgrimage route? Gwen worried that she might have a heart condition and expressed canceling our trip. (Needless to say, plane tickets had already been purchased and rooms booked.) I didn't want to entertain the thought of canceling. And yet if our problems continued unresolved we faced great risks, not to mention discomfort, pain and/or worry. Our worst fantasies brought up the possibility of a medical emergency in a foreign country. Fear and anxiety, our ever present friends, rose up to be challenged.

Within the context of a pilgrimage that honors the Goddess of Compassion one had to ask whether Kannon, our own inner nature, had risen to push us into new territories of expansion. When my foot refused to heal, and the date of our trip grew ever closer, I had to find new levels of perseverance and determination within myself. I had to overcome my focus of self-concern in order to honor my commitment or vow to finish what

I had started. The power of the devotional path of pilgrimage brought all that needed purifying to the fore—fear, anxiety, selfishness, irritation, impatience, anger, resentment.... We had set something sacred in motion and it wanted to complete itself. Compassionate action for ourselves and others could only move us closer to our own spiritual unfolding. Yet Kannon's "gift" had not elicited any feeling of gratitude.

Three weeks before our departure date my foot had improved, but walking any significant distance without pain eluded me. Gwen's PVCs had diminished and her test results didn't reveal any serious coronary issues. Neither of us talked about canceling the trip. Rather we resolved to accept whatever life had in store for us. We surrendered to the power of the pilgrimage and Kannon's guiding wisdom.

Zen master Daehaeng Sunim, a teacher in the Korean tradition, said, "Although it may not seem like it at the time, later you will realize that the suffering you are experiencing is actually Buddhas and bodhisattvas who have come to purify you and help you grow."

A glimmer of understanding came to the fore, yet I still resisted the idea of being in pain. Alas, two days before departure and right when I needed a shot of wisdom, a Zen teacher e-mailed me the "Liberation from All Obstructions" chant. Line number five says: "If there's pain, I choose to feel." I vowed to dedicate the pain of my sore foot toward the alleviation of suffering of all sentient beings. Now my discomfort had a greater purpose.

* * *

By the time we arrived in Japan, I had crossed many mental hurdles that prepare one for pilgrimage. Phil Cousineau's *The Art of Pilgrimage* lay by my bedside with this passage tabbed, "... the medieval Japanese believed that the sorrows of travel were challenges to overcome and transform into poetry and song."

At 3:50 AM I sat up in bed wide awake and eager to read the chapter entitled, "The Moment of Truth"; it began with a quote by Zen teacher John Daido Loori: "If you miss the moment, you miss your life."

With that, I got up, got dressed and, per my physical therapist's instructions, happily taped my foot. An ibuprofen and a prayer at each meal promised to get me through the next phase of our pilgrimage.

Chapter 21

Passing through the fields
On a mountain path
Heading towards rainy skies
From Yoshimine
The evening showers clear

Yoshiminidera – Temple 20

The Fire Brothers of Purification

High above Kyoto in the surrounding mountains, Yoshiminidera looks down upon the city with a raven's view—detached, lofty, a bit removed from the human fray. Pathways meander up and around the mountain with shrines and ponds and icons at every bend. The many beautiful statues brought me into relationship with Kannon, Medicine Buddha, Amida, the Five Acala Fire Deities, Priest Genzan (the founder) and Lady Keishoin—the main benefactress of Yoshiminidera after its devastation from civil war in the 15th century.

Autumn reds and golds—barely beginning to show on the November day of our visit—coupled with sunny skies made for a pleasant scramble up steep paths past glassy ponds. The last remaining Japanese anemone, its delicate white petals against a back drop of greenish pond water and rough moss-covered stone, delighted as much as the historical statues and stunning views, or for that matter the pine tree whose two branches had been trained to grow as long arms (72 and 78 feet respectively) from a thick stunted trunk. The tree, over 600 years old, had witnessed thousands of pilgrims standing in the same spot where I stood. They too admired, commented, marveled and speculated on this unique specimen nicknamed Pine of the Frolicking Dragon. My life span in comparison—a short blip in its presence and much shorter than the 300-year-old cherry and maple that shared this temple compound—humbled me. I made an imaginary bow to these elders. And yet, even they, with their centuries-old bodies, would someday perish.

Kannon's presence, the manifestation of physical beauty found in plants, trees, stones and rarified air, could be felt throughout this complex, sometimes called the Temple of the Pine. Although the magnificent Pine didn't outshine a lone Beauty Berry hidden behind the Buddha Hall; its arching branches lush with purple berries filled our cameras with more shots than the Frolicking Dragon. As tea and ikebana practitioners, Beauty Berry conjured images of tea houses, tea ceremony, quietude and elegance. In Japan, the *Callicarpa japonica* is called *murasakishikubu* in honor of Lady Murasaki, (the author of the Tale of Genji), and Murasaki the character, (Genji's amour)—*murasaki* being the word for purple. The fact that trees and flowers and bushes in Japanese culture often had stories, symbolism, legends and layers of meaning wrapped around them, made every aspect of nature, no matter how seemingly insignificant, come alive in ways deeper than the physical appearance itself.

From Beauty Berry to vermillion torii gates to sutra halls, I limped along with a little help from my painkiller friend. Prayers and petitions, made at all the usual places for others, somehow never got directed at myself. Was I really that altruistic? Or would I rather not know if personal, spontaneous healing really worked? If I prayed for some distant person, some abstraction, I would never know whether my prayers were effective or not. And if my prayer wasn't answered would I lose faith? Would I think prayer a waste of time? Whatever the answer, I decided then and there to appeal to the Fire Deities, represented at Yoshiminidera as the Five Acala (Immovable) Deities housed in a special temple called the Goma-do, or Fire Hall. And if that didn't work I would request a healing for myself at Anaoji—the next temple on our itinerary—known for its healing miracles.

In Shingon and Tendai Buddhism, wrathful deities, often surrounded by rings of fire and carrying a sword, figured prominently into the Buddhist story of enlightenment. Their faces evoked a stern, fierce, and wrathful countenance in stark contrast to the peaceful, serene poses we see on Kannon's or Buddha's face. Their swords represent the wisdom that cuts through ignorance and delusion. Fire, one of the Six Great Elements, has powerful symbolic meaning. Fire burns up things—things like negative karma, ill deeds, bad thoughts, delusions, false views, hindrances... Throw them all in the fire, give them over to the Fire Deity, let him purify you of all your misguided thoughts and deeds. With fire, everything unwanted could be gotten rid of quickly. No trace left behind. Maybe a puff of smoke, but it too would quickly dissolve through the element of Wind.

In the Goma Ceremony, fire is our friend, our Myo'o, the higher wisdom of the True Self, the servant of Buddha taking care of business. Nothing meek here. Meekness had its place, but sometimes we needed wrath, we needed benevolent force to stand up to the intractable delusions of anger, hatred, irritation, fear, anxiety, worry... Let the Fire God consume it. Poof! It's gone. No more years and years of grappling with that demon. Feed it to Acala. Let him dine on your neurosis, your deluded thoughts, your negativities, your ignorance.

We left Yoshiminidera via a steep pathway that led back to the main road. Still able to walk, although not comfortably, I felt lighthearted anyway knowing that I had successfully made it to my first temple, toured the entire grounds, walked up the steep stone stairs and back down again, and now had made it to the bus stop.

On the way back to Kyoto we passed a garden filled with deep red cockscomb (a gentler reminder of fire); they made me think of the haiku poet Masaoka Shiki, but I couldn't remember why. Later, when I researched his controversial haiku—cockscomb/ I'm sure there are at least/fourteen or fifteen stalks—it wasn't the haiku itself that struck me, but the fact that he viewed these red, fire-like flowers from his sick bed and died at the age of 35. We could feed everything to the Fire God, sacrifice everything on the altar of beauty, and still we would perish well before the Pine, the Maple and the Cherry. My time to shine like the delicate anemone was running out.

Had I surrendered anything? I still resisted the pain in my foot, still sought comfort over discomfort, still wanted to be secure and warm and healthy. Although later, I imagined with great delight feeding all my fears and misguided thoughts to the Fire Deity. He consumed them in one big hot gulp, and for a few moments, peace descended.

Chapter 22

In the next world
I may be born again
To more human suffering
So I pray
With ten voices, one voice

Anaoji – Temple 21

Buddha Entering Nirvana

From Kyoto Enmachi Station we boarded a train headed for Kameoka, and before long disappeared in and out of one train tunnel after another, each time emerging into rugged, almost wild, mountain terrain with green-blue rivers tumbling through deep rocky gorges—darkness then light, then darkness; in the tunnel out of the tunnel; now a pine forest, now bamboo, now a pristine stream. Take it in quick before it gets dark again. I wanted the train to stop so I could get out and explore this wild area, absorb these natural wonders, revel for awhile. And the train did stop in some obscure outpost where five men got off with their backpacks and scrambled down a path alongside the train trellis. I wanted to tag along. But we were on pilgrimage, headed for a small neighborhood temple called Anaoji known for its reclining Buddha (or Buddha entering nirvana) famous for healing; then I remembered my foot. Oh yeah, I couldn't go hiking even if I wanted to.

This time I would not only ask for healing, but insist on it. I had been putting up with this foot injury for almost six months now. I wanted it to stop. I wanted to go hiking like those men, strong and carefree on my feet. I firmly believed that instant cures and miracle healings had validity. Since, in theory, no separation existed between myself and Kannon, health and harmony of all my body parts seemed possible and right. If healing didn't happen, well then I had to keep surrendering to the process.

"If there's pain, I choose to feel."

Had I already been willing to toss this wisdom teaching aside for immediate gratification? I tried to find the balance between acceptance and resignation, surrender and pro-activity, humility and self-worth.

Okay, I would ask, that's all. I would rub the foot of the Buddha and ask for a healing.

With a little envy, I watched the men disappear into a thicket before the train moved on into another tunnel. When we emerged, the vista opened to a wide valley filled with rice fields and vegetable gardens—the healthiest, bushiest, greenest vegetable gardens ever.

From train to bus, we careened down narrow streets and windy roads through fields of cosmos dotted with trellises laden with blue morning glory. Golden rod, or solidago, heavy with autumn color, warmed the empty spaces along the roadside. The plentiful plumes brought me back to childhood when my mother collected golden rod and other plants from the prairie to create dried-flower arrangements. Half way across the world on another continent, golden rod mixed with memories of my past. Mother would have been surprised to know that the Japanese prized these wild plants as much as she did.

The bus dropped us a block from Anaoji even though our guidebook indicated a ten-minute walk. Delighted for my foot, I made an extra deep bow before the temple gate and stopped to examine the once bright red Nio. Over time their paint had peeled and dulled, but the two guardians, ferocious and wrathful, still guarded the temple from all misfortune and negativity.

Upon entering the Anaoji grounds, the special quality of this place began to reveal itself in subtle ways. Two women wearing simple cotton aprons and head scarves swept leaves from stones and walkways. Instead of the usual gas powered leaf blowers, the swooshing sound of their bamboo brooms settled into my psyche like soothing background music.

Our guide book said that Temple 21 had little of interest. Quite the contrary. Like many of the smaller, less known temples along the pilgrimage, Anaoji had a special feeling of welcome mixed with quiet simplicity. From the minute we crossed the threshold this temple enveloped us in its humble presence.

The first noticeable difference: everyone was female—the sweepers, the temple steward, the pavilion receptionist. The latter politely accepted our 500 yen admittance to see the Teian garden and other treasures.

The Chinese style garden, designed with stones that represented Amida's Pure Land and the 33 manifestations of Kannon laid out in the Lotus Sutra, was a point of contemplation from the sun filled verandah. The viewing platform overlooked the pond with a distant view of a two-story pagoda in the background. I tried to locate the 33 stones around the pond that represented Kannon, but my eye kept returning to the brilliant green moss-covered bridge that crossed to the other side, to the Pure Land. Ah, if it could be as simple as stepping onto that bridge!

Inside the pavilion, the various rooms had been outfitted with ikebana or *chabana*, scrolls, painted screens and ceramic incense burners. Each corner or alcove provided a place for appreciation and reflection. On the other side of the pavilion, up a slanting wood corridor that entered the back of the hondo, lay Shakyamuni Buddha in the reclining pose. Carved in the 13th century, this Buddha had been rubbed smooth by the thousands of hands that had touched his body parts in hopes of a cure. I awaited my miracle healing with anticipation.

We entered the cold, dark hondo and found Buddha under a pink quilt. He left this world lying on his right side with one foot over the other and his head propped up on his right hand. His last words to his disciples, "View the dharma as an island. Do not seek refuge elsewhere." He gave them a chance to ask questions, but they remained silent. Then he promised that they would all realize enlightenment and reminded them of the impermanence of all things. With those final words he passed into that state of perfect, timeless peace where all suffering has ended.

I lifted the corner of the quilt so I could rub Buddha's right foot. I rubbed his left one too for good measure. Gwen rubbed his chest, the place over his heart. The custom to donate a quilt to the temple when you've been cured of your ailment ensured that reclining Buddha, like a magical sleeping baby, always had a new quilt.

The feminine characteristics of Anaoji pervaded this small neighborhood temple with a kind of innocent sweetness. Everything was done with care, quiet, and affection. Even the depositing of my copied Heart Sutras elicited a kind, smiling, affirmative response. The surrounding community obviously took much pride in their historical neighborhood temple, a little gem in the middle of rice, radish and cosmos fields. And yet despite the loving, healing feelings so apparent at this temple, only a handful of pilgrims toured the grounds. Three men with small worn prayer books stood outside the hondo and together chanted the Heart Sutra. After they finished I silently repeated the same sutra in English and recited 108 mantras on my mala. The ideas of "form and emptiness," especially emptiness as form, made me pause periodically to view a scene, any scene, mundane or poetically beautiful with new perspective. Buddha too had appeared as form, a man named Prince Siddhartha who became Shakyamuni Buddha. And just as our form will dissolve into emptiness so too did his. Reclining Buddha or Buddha entering nirvana is Buddha Shakyamuni's death pose—an ordinary human being who succumbed to food poisoning, even though psychically he foresaw this event months in advance and did nothing to avert it.

The day after rubbing Healing/Reclining Buddha's foot I

had the thought that fear was trapped in my heel. The tape I'd wrapped under my arch for support now felt like foot binding — oppressive. Was I trying to avoid the pain? The tape irritated my skin and caused two raw blisters. I undid the tape to release my foot, to let it out of its trap. I wanted to let go of fear. By the middle of that day, I walked longer distances with ease. By the end of the day, the pain felt minimal. Was Healing Buddha imparting an insight through my own intuitive cognitive process so that I could release the dis-ease in my body? And my next thought: if I'm healed, how will I send him a quilt?

The following day the pain in my heel returned. I had not been the recipient of a miracle, but I did feel that something psychological had shifted — an awareness, a letting go process. With each step I repeated "let go," "let it all go," and the "Liberation from All Obstructions" chant played out: "May all Buddhas and wise ones help me live this now."

Chapter 23

There is no one
Old or young
Who cannot rely upon
Kannon's vow of help
At Sojiji

Sojiji – Temple 22

Honoring the Animal Realm

The pet cemetery, turtle story, turtles and animal amulets found at Temple 22 make this small neighborhood temple especially dear for animal lovers, pet owners and anyone who cares about, sympathizes with, or advocates for the plight of animals. Although not as charming in the old ancient way, Sojiji has many beautiful enclaves with black pine providing dramatic outlines around stone lanterns and large boulders. A new temple with a clean, modern feel, the shrine to Benzaiten, goddess of all that flows, sits on the back of a gigantic stone and cement turtle in the middle of a pond. Fat koi lazily move around the turtle statue. Two basketball size dragon heads at the bottom of the pond spew water in opposite directions. A dozen small *live* turtles bask on a nearby boulder. Everything animate and inanimate exudes contentment.

A sunny and warm November day, Gwen found the pond and garden a perfect place to rest and compose haiku:

fall color —
found mostly
in the koi

I went about picture snapping and mantra chanting; then

meandered over to the ever present *Mizuko Jizo* and the very rare pet cemetery. On my way back to the pond, I stopped at the shrine of 88 Buddha statues representing the 88 temples of the Shikoku pilgrimage—each deity carved with a unique expression. In the middle of all these Buddhas stood a tall black Bokefuji Kannon giving protection against senile dementia, and making Sojiji one of the Bokefuji pilgrimage stops in addition to the Saigoku pilgrimage.

With the special emphasis on compassion for animals, and the founding story of how a Fujiwara nobleman purchased a turtle about to be slaughtered and released it in the nearby river, I wanted to know more about Life Release, the Buddhist practice of saving an animal from an untimely death.

The impetus behind Life Release most likely originated from stories about Buddha's great compassion for animals. One such story tells of Prince Siddhartha (before he became Buddha Shakyamuni) as a boy, growing up in India. On an outing in the forest of the vast palace grounds, his cousin Devadatta wanted to try out his new bow and arrow by shooting a swan. The arrow found its intended target and the swan fell from the sky. Siddhartha, seeing what his cousin had done, ran ahead concerned only for the fate of the swan. He found it lying on the ground, still alive, with Devadatta's arrow in its wing. Devadatta wanted to claim the swan for himself, but Prince Siddhartha wanted to nurse the swan back to health by applying medicinal herbs to its wound. An argument ensued. Both boys wanted the swan. To decide the fate of the magnificent bird they went to see a wise old sage. After hearing the story, the sage told the boys that all creatures wanted to live and be happy, and therefore the swan should be in the care of the one who tried to save its life not the one who tried to take it.

The practitioner of Life Release or Animal Release, finds, buys, or rescues an animal that is in harm's way or designated to be killed or slaughtered; thus saving the animal's life. If it is a wild animal, then it should be native to the region where it is released so that it can easily survive in that particular climate and geography. If it is a domestic animal, it should be raised in an appropriate place or given to a farm sanctuary, or in the case of a cat or dog, cared for in your home.

The down side of Life Release rituals and ceremonies is that some entrepreneurs have learned how to exploit other's acts of compassion to make a profit. They capture animals in the wild and take them into the cities where they know devoted Buddhists will buy them for big money. Once released, they repeat the cycle.

In Myanmar, children at major well-visited temples, catch small birds, keep them confined in tiny bamboo cages and sell them to tourists to be released. Once freed, the children recapture and resell the birds over and over in a never ending cycle. In these cases, it may be more meritorious not to buy the animal or bird rather than reward a practice that has no benefit to the animal at all, and may even harm them. (Of course people resort to such extreme measures out of unrelenting poverty, but that's another matter entirely.)

Due to Life Release practices, some non-native species have been unknowingly introduced into the environment, not only harming the habitat, but the animal too. Perhaps the fish, reptile or animal needs certain foods, weather conditions, temperatures (hotter or colder) in order to survive. Saving the life of an animal that cannot adapt to its new environment could result in the animal dying prematurely—perhaps from starvation, hypothermia, or new predators—not an act of compassion.

Life Release is carried out today by Buddhists throughout Asia and the Western world. In Taiwan, even Catholics and Protestants have taken it up.

But we don't need to buy exotic or non-exotic animals to express our empathy for living beings. One easy act of kindness that anyone can do without spending extra money or leaving home or trying to figure out what to do with a sheep or cow is to reduce or eliminate the eating of meat and fish. Since most animals slaughtered for human consumption are raised these days in "factory farms" with horrific conditions, the act of becoming a vegetarian is one of the most compassionate actions one can do for the animal kingdom in general. But even here, in Buddha's wisdom, no sweeping commandment strictly forbids the eating of meat. Rather, he suggested abstaining from harming other sentient beings as much as possible. He said this so that those who, for whatever reason, be it dietary needs, economic necessity or geographical limitation, could not be a complete vegetarian would not be riddled with guilt, remorse or bad feelings. Better to have Right Intention, be sincere, and free your mind of negativity.

In Buddha's day, and even now in many countries, monks and nuns go on begging rounds. Out of gratitude, they eat whatever is put in their bowl, which in some cases might be meat or fish. The animal protein is not refused, but eaten prayerfully, acknowledging where it comes from, asking to be worthy of the sustenance.

If we have to eat meat, we can give thanks to the animal for nourishing our body and ask that we be worthy of taking a life so that we may live. We can vow to use our life for the liberation of all beings.

Before I left for Japan I requested a healing for my foot from a Tibetan Rinpoche. He suggested reciting Medicine Buddha mantras and prayers and saving the lives of animals to increase my merit and purify negative actions done in the past. I could buy an animal at a live animal market (apparently there are hundreds of such markets in the U.S. alone), or I could donate money to an animal rescue organization or sanctuary, or I could send a donation to a special fish releasing ceremony performed in India.

Since my cardiologist recommends eating fish, and I

occasionally did, the least hypocritical action would be refraining from eating seafood even while in the land of sushi and sashimi. I also donated money to Posada, an animal rescue organization in my home state. These practices, coupled with our visit to Sojiji and learning of its founding legend, provided an opportunity to revisit Right Action, to once again go to the heart of compassion for all living things and to tread a little lighter, a little more mindfully in the world of all creatures great and small. I had been justifying the eating of fish for heart reasons, but the latest research on food and health suggested that a completely plant based diet offered superior benefit. When I read that Buddha Shakyamuni carried a staff to scare away insects and thus prevent stepping on them, I knew I had a long way to go.

When Takafusa Fujiwara saved the turtle from being slaughtered little did he know that his act of compassion would immediately return to him. The very next day his son's step-mother threw him into the river. When Fujiwara-san prayed to Kannon for his son's safety the turtle appeared. He swam under the boy's body and carried him to the bank thus saving his life. The grateful father vowed to build a temple to honor Kannon. Over many years, and many twists and turns of fate, this land gave birth to Sojiji, a place where today, twelve centuries later, people come to honor and respect the animal realm. The story of the released turtle who rescued the boy may or may not be true, but the story redirects our mind back to compassion and helps visitors to Sojiji evaluate their karmic actions in relationship to animals. Temple 22 forces us to consider the merit of bestowing acts of kindness on every living creature we meet, and of creating a safer and more loving world for all beings.

I suspected that the turtle moms, dads and babies lazily enjoying the autumn sun in Benzaiten's pond had been mercifully saved from becoming *suppon nabe* a hot bubbling pot of turtle soup or stew. Turtle, considered medicinal and of the highest quality, has been eaten in Japan since ancient days when it was prized among the royal household. Even today, turtle meat, a rare and expensive delicacy only the rich can afford, is still slaughtered and eaten without any thought for the animal's life.

The turtles basking on the rock looked content being live turtles. They moved languidly, soaked up the warmth, occasionally went for a swim, and jostled for a prime spot in the sun, much like humans do at the beach. It turns out that turtles, like us, just want to be happy.

Chapter 24

Although heavy with sin
In the teachings
Of Katsuoji
My burden will be lightened
When I pray to Kannon

Katsuoji – Temple 23

Bodhidharma Comes to Japan

Opening to another pilgrimage experience, we purified at Katsuoji's temizuya and headed over a wide bridge that crossed Benzaiten's pond. Temple 23 and the goddess of all that flows welcomed us with unusual and unexpected billowing mists. Every few seconds, underwater jets spewed water into the air, which created clouds of breath-like steam. True to her reputation, the deity of arts and locution inspired poetic reverie as we took our time crossing the bridge to revel in her "healing vapors." In the early morning air the sun illuminated distant landscapes, then disappeared behind clouds of steam rising up from the pond, obscuring tree shapes and other solid objects as if lost in a dream.

Once deposited on the other side, the steep stone stairs transported us toward the upper level temple compound. Before reaching the first tier of steps, loudspeakers hidden throughout the tree tops amplified the chanting of sutras to the accompaniment of taiko-like drums. I couldn't decide if the "loudspeaker sutras" added or detracted from the ambience, but this is what Sister had to say:

loudspeaker sutras —
call to compassion
for the hard of hearing

The dramatic chanting and drumming brought us up to the second tier of steps to admire the gazillions of bright red rounded Darumas, the caricatured head of the beloved Zen patriarch Bodhidharma. Sometimes called the "Blue-Eyed Barbarian," Bodhidharma traveled from Southern India in the 5th or 6th century to bring Chan Buddhism to China. Chan, or Zen, wouldn't take root in Japan until another six hundred years.

Bodhidharma, surrounded by folklore and legend, supposedly meditated for nine years in a cave located in Northern China, a region with cold snowy winters. Said to have cut off his eyelids to keep from falling asleep during long periods of meditation, the eyelids that fell to the ground purportedly gave rise to the first tea plants—the stimulating drink that helped monks and nuns stay alert during long meditation periods. The absent eyelids may explain why Daruma dolls are depicted with a wide-open stare. Darumas, with their bright red color and association with a holy man, also became a talisman in 18th-century Japan for warding off smallpox. With the introduction of the smallpox vaccination, the ritual of coloring in one eye, making a wish, and coloring in the other after the wish was granted, transferred to good luck in general—whether it be obtaining a job, passing a test, finding a suitable partner, winning an election, getting pregnant, or anything else humans desired for their happiness. Some temples also conduct eye-painting ceremonies for Daruma dolls. In these ceremonies a monk (for a small donation) will paint the blank left eye with the Sanskrit sound for "A." If the wish is fulfilled the Sanskrit sound for "N" is drawn in. These two symbols have the same meaning as the sounds uttered by the Nio or protectors of Buddhism found at the front gate of all Buddhist temples throughout Japan; "Ah" and "Un," (the equivalent of the Sanskrit "Aum" or "Om"), the beginning and end, the alpha and omega.

At Katsuoji, as elsewhere, Daruma is associated with attainment. He epitomized someone who exhibited extreme diligence, discipline and forbearance—qualities deemed worthy of cultivation. Bodhidharma then became a kind of dharma role model, much more useful than remembering his legend or proving whether he really did cut off those eyelids. Fantastical narratives sometimes overshadowed underlying messages and the deeper symbolism of icons meant to point toward the inner reality that each of us possessed. Bodhidharma, like Kannon and all the other deities, was not meant to be worshipped "out there," but to symbolize a quality, state of being, or aspect of each person's potential. We went to "sacred places" to be reminded, to be brought back to ourselves.

Temple 23 has become a repository of hundreds of little Daruma dolls and countless larger dolls with both left and right eyes colored in. Daruma dolls line temple walls, gates, gardens, the bell tower, the pond, and even the center of two bronze lotus blossoms flanking Mizuko Kannon at the front entrance. In keeping with tradition we couldn't pass up buying our own Darumas and making a wish. I wished for that elusive state of liberation for myself and others, a state of peace that someday might be reflected as outer peace, world peace. A lofty wish, yes, but why not reach for the highest?

Daruma dolls and wish-granting talisman's aside, Daruma, or Bodhidharma, more than "winner's luck," symbolizes the Right Effort of the Eightfold Path, the determination to apply oneself to seeing through the ignorance of our own mind, of maximizing this opportunity called "precious human life." Although cutting off one's eyelids—a rather dramatic overstatement of that determination—no doubt had its place as an encouragement story. Even so, I felt inspired by Bodhidharma's single pointed effort to triumph over the limitations of the human mind.

A strong proponent of the teachings on emptiness, or lack of inherent existence, the direct path to enlightenment, Bodhidharma dismissed ritual, sutra chanting, ascetic practices and so called meritorious deeds. A story recounts that he told

Emperor Wu, a devout Buddhist of his day famous for building numerous temples, that doing so had no merit. Merit, in Buddhism, results from performing good deeds which in turn off-sets negative karma, but one has to have Right Intention, and not wish to gain anything for oneself. The Emperor's motivation under institutionalized Buddhism may have been questionable or compromised; therefore resulting in "no merit," or perhaps Bodhidharma wanted to stress the importance of rigorous meditation practice over other activities.

Rather than earning "merit," Bodhidharma's best advice: don't look for Buddha outside your own mind. Buddha, not to be confused with a person or a statue, was a state of mind— awareness itself; and everyone had Buddha-nature. To prostrate in front of icons, or recite sutras or perform other Buddhist rituals was secondary to meditation or watching one's mind. The important point was to penetrate the illusion that Buddhahood resided out there, outside one's own True Self. He would say that, "the mind is the Buddha, and the Buddha is the mind. Beyond the mind there is no Buddha, and beyond the Buddha there is no mind."

Bodhidharma preached a radical view that challenged the existing institution of Buddhism in China. He had a large following and may have ruffled too many fundamentalist feathers with his direct and unadorned approach to enlightenment. A 13th-century account of his life and death proclaims that his fellow monks may have systematically poisoned him. But this account has not been verified any more than other stories surrounding the legend of Bodhidharma. Three years after his supposed death, a government official encountered Bodhidharma in the mountains. He walked quickly with one sandal in his hand. When the official asked where he was going Bodhidharma said, "To India." No doubt shocked when such news reached the offending monks, they opened his tomb to verify the story. Only a lone sandal remained—or so the story goes. Needless to say,

Bodhidharma's legend, shrouded in mystery, made an indelible impact in the world of Zen.

In our haste toward catching the last bus of the day, we missed the "Circle of Wisdom," a stone pathway surrounding two upright monolithic-like rocks, a kind of oracle that provides a place to access insight and clarify life's challenges. As we made our way toward the exit, I looked back and saw a young couple intently traversing its pathway, anticipating, no doubt, the answer to whatever secret questions haunted them. What would I have asked of the wisdom circle? I couldn't conjure any burning metaphysical questions, only the self-focused thought of how to heal my foot injury—a question that had elicited numerous and varied answers, none of which had provided the cure.

Across the road from the temple, a very steep stone staircase—the old pilgrim's path—disappeared high up into the thickness of mountain foliage. With my foot pain stirred up from temple walking, exploring this path remained out of the question. Instead I took a photo and left with a feeling of missed opportunity, a yearning to go deeply into the silence of the mountain and yet frustrated over the hindrance. The pathway, like so many in the sacred mountains of Japan, beckoned. That call, no other than the wish to enter into the interior of my own being, my own mysterious essence, pressed upon me. Not being able to follow the physical metaphor felt incomplete, yet I knew, at least intellectually, that nothing prevented me from knowing that deep place other than my own lack of fortitude on the spiritual path.

Still, I did not have a Bodhidharma disposition: the definitive pilgrim. He left his familiar country and spent years at sea in order to take the dharma to a foreign land. His unshakeable realization and conviction towered over my petty obsession with foot pain and bus schedules. In that I had to accept my own limitations. The steep stone stairs lay ahead, enticing, foreboding, mysterious, alluring, but not yet completely doable. Mundane, practical considerations dictated our day. In retrospect, I regretted making the compromise, but felt thankful for the overall experience of pilgrimage and the chance to visit temples that most foreigners would never venture out to see.

We left Katsuoji over the same mist-shrouded bridge, and like a satisfying dream that lingers long into the morning, Benzaiten's blessings left an imprint of peace and joy. But what of all those red Daruma doll heads with wide open eyes? Bodhidharma would have had a good laugh at the craziness of a world that would turn him into a good luck talisman. I could hear his scoffing tone, "No merit. No merit."

Chapter 25

Passing through
Fields and villages
I'm going on to
The Temple of Nakayama
To pray for the next life

Nakayamadera – Temple 24

Celebrating Life

Children in kimono posing for their parents' cameras, and children in bright yellow hats out for the day with their teachers, bobbed, bubbled, and skipped their way through the many shrines of Middle Mountain Temple (Temple 24). Every worship "station," bedecked with either pots of flowers in brilliant hues, strings of pastel colored folded cranes, or traditional designs in fresh coats of paint, exuded aliveness. The children and the flowers and the brilliant colors made this one of the most cheerful and lively temples on the pilgrimage—even though an underlying layer held the grief and sadness of many departed "water babies" and young lives.

The newly constructed temple halls painted vermillion and decorated with dragon, cloud, chrysanthemum and geometric pattern motifs replicated how these temples would have looked hundreds of years ago, before wind, rain and time ate away the colorful artistry.

The Gohyaku Rakan-do, or Hall of 500 Disciples of Buddha Shakyamuni mesmerized with 500 one-of-a-kind depictions. Every face contained its own unique personality. And for once, they didn't forget the women. Buddha's female disciples stood side by side with their male counterparts. How refreshing! Yet, true to form, the first tier of disciples, the larger prominent ones, were all male.

The steep stone stairs, although few in number, created a sense of ease, an absence of struggle and effort. Perhaps a trek to the inner sanctuary, a snake infested area higher up on the mountain would have dispelled the lightheartedness of this temple experience, but that was blocked off the day of our visit, so that only the lower part of the temple remained accessible.

Nakayamadera, once considered the "center of paradise" and Temple 1 on the Kannon pilgrimage, has a reputation for bestowing safe childbirth upon its devotees. One could also pray for the souls of one's enemies here. Per many a legend in Japan, the founding of a sacred site came about through a vision. In this case, Prince Shotoku, a legendary figure in Japanese history, wandered through these mountains near Osaka when he saw a "purple cloud" no less, hovering over Nakayama (the middle mountain of a group of three). He built a temple on this site to honor and pray for the souls of the departed.

Yet today, Nakayamadera presents, not only a memorial for the young lives taken too soon, but a celebration of the lives they might have had. The two energies worked synergistically and created an atmosphere of timelessness between birth and death and yet encompassed both. In the end my vote went for life. Life should be celebrated, relished and enjoyed while it lasted. Live vibrantly, wildly, said the colors; live joyfully and kindly, said the pots of cyclamen, pansies and begonias; live elegantly with refinement, said the large displays of King and Spider chrysanthemums. But don't forget that it's all impermanent said the Kofun tomb, an ancient burial site from the 2nd century thought to be the final resting place of Empress Onaka. The bibed Jizos spoke of the anguish of miscarriage and abortion; and the ropes of thousands of cranes spoke of premature death, war atrocities, and a young girl's courage. Follow the Way of the Buddha said the 500 disciples. Find your own true self and stop seeking; it is here now manifesting as all these myriad forms. Celebrate! Celebrate!

Chapter 26

Such feeling!
Around every corner
And in every place
There is nothing it misses —
The waves of this pure water

Kiyomizudera – Temple 25

The False Buddhist

A steep windy bus ride, or a steep uphill climb, either one will get you to the top of Mt. Mitake and the second Kiyomizu temple on the pilgrimage (the first and most famous being Temple 16 in Kyoto). The most striking feature of Temple 25's compound is the mountain itself — remote, lofty, and filled with tall cedars, lacy maples and stately gingkos. In autumn the maples turn shades of red, burgundy, orange, rust, and yellow; the gingkos a deep golden yellow.

Craggy old stone stairs, the original pilgrim's route, can take you higher into the lofty regions of the mountain or down lower, toward the foothills. Due to my foot injury and the scarcity of returning buses (only two per day), I didn't do either, and only imagined what delights lay ahead up one of those foreboding crumbling staircases built so many centuries ago. Other than the hindrance of my ongoing foot pain, the lingering memory of my visit to Kiyomizudera was not my inability to partake in the old pilgrim's path, but a spontaneous conversation that sprang up with a fellow pilgrim, a Japanese woman who wanted to practice her English.

I'm usually quite accommodating when someone from the culture where I'm a guest attempts to converse with me in my language. But the implication that arose during a brief conversation with *this* fellow pilgrim, the presumption that I was not a "real" Buddhist because I came from a Western country, a Christian country (she assumed that I was Christian) and didn't know how to chant the goeikas as she did, gave me pause for thought. It was a bit disheartening to have come all this way, all the way across the Pacific Ocean, all the way from Kyoto, all the way up this mountain from bus to train to bus, all the way up the steep stone stairs with an aching foot to the highest worship hall, to be labeled as someone less authentic, less devoted, less "real."

And yet, perhaps another layer that gave me pause had something to do with my own doubt. Was I a real Buddhist? Was I really embarking on this pilgrimage as a devotional journey to understand the phenomena of Kannon, the Goddess of Mercy? Was I really planting seeds of peace and awakening into the collective unconscious? I couldn't discount the literary possibilities, the adventure, the novelty of a pilgrimage in Japan, yet had to ask, what was/is a real Buddhist? With all my desires and attachments, judgments and opinions, could I call myself a Buddhist? Was Buddha a Buddhist? He didn't found a religion and all the accompanying forms and rituals. He didn't transcribe his teachings, or author goeikas. Some scriptures even say that the Buddha remained silent after his enlightenment and didn't teach at all. Buddha, as Prince Siddhartha, simply left the world of mundane, self-centered materialism found in his father's palace, to find truth—his truth, the way out of suffering. But even this story is refuted in the Lotus Sutra, which suggests that Buddha was already enlightened and merely played out a predestined script to show The Way. Who knew the real truth about the life of the Buddha, or the absolute true teachings of Buddhism? Most of what we know was written down by his disciples after Buddha's passing into nirvana, and then embellished, expanded or reinterpreted as Buddhism moved from culture to culture. In Japan, Buddhism, like all religions throughout the world, had a dark side. In addition to "warrior monks," in *Zen at War*, Brian

Daizen Victoria, tells the story of how institutional Buddhism in Japan contributed to the nationalistic fervor preceding World War II. Was a bit of this nationalism still lingering here? Was that Buddhist?

A curt, "Nice meeting you," rather abruptly ended any further potential for cultural misunderstanding between me and my fellow Japanese pilgrim. In self-defense, I silently argued that Buddha Shakyamuni was not born in Japan—or America for that matter. Both countries had imported a religion and philosophy that came from somewhere else, a country (India) that now wasn't Buddhist either, but Hindu. Who owned Buddhism? Who could own Buddha's realization of the Four Noble Truths: that life was suffering; that suffering was caused by desirous attachment; that these delusional states of mind could be overcome; and that there was a path leading to spiritual freedom.

Perhaps neither of us two pilgrims had a pure Buddhist mind, but I believed that we both aspired to that place. We had, for whatever reason, followed our heart's yearning and arrived on a mountain top Kannon temple as an act of devotion. Something had tugged at our spirit and we said "yes." "Real" or "not real" was irrelevant.

Yet as the day unfolded, I had to seriously ponder more than once: Was I a real Buddhist? I let the lure of material things (desire), the lure of a famous pottery village en route to Temple 25, distract and tantalize me with memories long past, a time when I first arrived in Japan 20 years previous and attended a pottery festival. The town had remained elusive, some unknown place off the beaten track, a place I thought I would never find again. And then, quite by accident, we discovered it on the way to Kiyomizudera. The bus traveled through the entire length of the town—Tachikui, home of Tamba pottery, famous for its "dragon" kiln (a wood-burning oven built up the side of a mountain), and renowned as one of the Six Ancient Kilns of Japan. Yes, this village, a true artisan's town of notable ceramic ware, shrouded in mystery and fond memories, beckoned this questionable Buddhist.

We could visit on our way back if we hurried and caught the second to last bus. It could drop us off in the town, and the last afternoon bus could pick us up. And so we performed our pilgrim's rituals, and left Kiyomizudera to revel, for a few hours, in the town of distant dream-like memory, in the ceramic art and the old ways of a Japanese craft town. I celebrated the artistic life, the simple life of the potter, and tried to forget about the troubling words of a fellow Buddhist who questioned my authenticity.

By the end of the long afternoon—my foot throbbing from too much walking, too much shopping, too much searching for the perfect vase in the perfect potter's town (a re-enactment of an old memory)—I was left with the impression of having been fooled yet again by the deceptive nature of desire. I had focused on an object/experience outside of myself, perceived it as the source of happiness, embellished its characteristics, pursued it, and experienced the result (not as satisfying as I had imagined)—a classic delusion of attachment, and manifestation of the second Noble Truth.

So perhaps my fellow pilgrim had been right: I wasn't a Buddhist (or at least not a very good one); just an ordinary being looking for a good time on a sunny autumn day in Japan— much like her I expect. Our one consolation lay in the chapter entitled "Skillful Means" found in the Lotus Sutra, where Buddha reassures Shariputra that all beings, no matter their imperfections will attain liberation:

Your hearts should be filled with great joy
For you know that you too will become Buddhas.

Chapter 27

In spring the cherry blossoms
In summer the orange blossoms
In autumn the chrysanthemum
Always exquisite—
The Way of the Mountain Flowers

Ichijoji – Temple 26

Water Babies

Information from SacredJapan.com talked about the Sai no Kawara, "a melancholy place with many cairns of stones and little Jizo statues, representing the shore of the River Sai where the spirits of departed children and babies gather." We could only surmise that it lay somewhere up the mountain now closed due to typhoon damage. We never found the cairns, but the story, the haunting tale of Sai no Kawara—a place and a story that has somehow inserted itself into Japanese Buddhism even though it is not Buddhist—goes like this:

When fetuses are aborted, or miscarry, or infants die suddenly, or children before the age of five die from disease or mishap, their spirits are said to reside in a kind of limbo or purgatory along the shore of a river. It is here that they pile up stones in order to create merit and climb out of this place of suffering so that they can eventually be transported to the Pure Land. But each night an evil hag sends her demons to the river bank to knock over the piles of stones. The next day, the children have to start all over again. In the midst of this hellish place, Jizo Bodhisattva in his compassion for the children helps them pile up their stones. Parents, friends, relatives or strangers can also help the children by piling up stones on earth as an act of atonement and remembrance on their behalf. The special

156

river bank or Sai no Kawara is this place in the Netherworld for departed souls of children and the not yet born. It is a sad place of tortured lingering, hardly any consolation for grieving parents. The story itself surely made up by some sadistic teller of tales.

Some temples take advantage of these old stories and superstitions by playing on parents' fears; thus garnering money for expensive services. The more compassionate aspect of these rituals provide consolation and an opportunity for parents to openly grieve and come to terms with their loss, feelings of guilt, or other emotions.

Not being able to find the cairns, we meandered back down to the bottom tier looking for other points of interest. We found the *mizuko* shrine, or Jizo-do, a somewhat neglected memorial to the water babies — stillborn, miscarried or aborted fetuses that have left the "waters" of the mother's womb for the "waters" of the great stream of life. No piled up stones, just the sweetest, the saddest and most unique Jizo-do I remember seeing.

Pinwheels, toys, stuffed animals, candy and anything and everything a young child might enjoy are interspersed among hundreds of miniature Jizo statues. Ropes of 1,000 origami cranes hang from the rafters. Above the Jizo-do are paintings depicting the bodhisattva's descent into hell where he rescued his mother and vowed to rescue all who suffer in the lower realms. The paintings depict the horrible tortures of hell, the miseries of the animal and human realms, and the final ascension to the peace and bliss of the Buddha realm. Jizo also vowed to protect women, travelers and children, which is why he is present at every children's cemetery, and children's memorial, and along every roadside and path and mountain hike, and why he is found in paintings and comics, and well, just about everywhere in Japan. After visiting the mizuko shrine Gwen wrote:

water babies' shrine —
only a few pinwheels
catch the breeze

At the end of our visit, while waiting for the bus (only 4 per day going, and 4 coming back) we sat inside a little café-like building across from the temple stocked with self-serve, complimentary tea. The Jizo shrine and all those pinwheels—some spinning, some not, some bright, some dulled by age, some bent, some straight, but all of them placed there in remembrance of a child that would never experience the magic of colors spinning in the wind—left a lingering feeling of sorrow in this already suffering world.

Chapter 28

Coming from so far away
As I climb Mt. Shosha
The sound of the wind
Rustling in the pines —
Isn't this the Dharma?

Engyoji – Temple 27

The Temple of Light Heartedness

Every temple has its own ambience or energy; its own slice of the Buddhist story. At Engyoji, the message emparted: Be Happy! Everyone exuded a warm, welcoming, cheerful, light and loving nature. Nobody seemed uptight here. The ticket takers, van drivers, other pilgrims—all exuded a cheerful demeanor. Many greeted us with *Konnichiwa*, and asked where we were from.

The temple, interspersed among ancient cedar trees on the top of Mt. Shosha, high above the city of Himeji, can easily be reached by cable car. The path to Engyoji, lined with 33 beautiful bronze Kannon statues, mimics the actual pilgrimage in miniature.

Three groups of children streamed through the temple complex on the day of our visit, all of them dressed in school uniforms of blue, yellow, green, and white with colorful caps. The color of the cap identified the individual groups. There were the orange caps and the blue caps and the white caps.

The children, bedecked in their bright colors, looked like little chirpy parakeets going up and down the steep stone stairs. Well-behaved, they followed their teachers without any fuss. I didn't see anyone pushing or shoving or bullying or creating any kind of stir or disruption. They too were simply happy, and so I wrote:

everywhere
throughout Engyoji
autumn flowers blooming

It is said that anyone who climbs this mountain will be purified in body and spirit. Although we all arrived by cable car rather than by foot, once we reached the clear lofty heights under autumn's color, I sensed the purifying effects; and as a woman, I felt lucky to be able to tour this temple complex at the top of Mt. Shosha without any special permission or passes. In the days of Izumi Shikibu, the mountain was forbidden to all women. Even the Lady herself, a great admirer of the priest Shoku, was not allowed to visit him at Engyoji. Instead, they exchanged poetry. After hearing the story recounted in the Lotus Sutra whereby the young daughter of the Dragon King attained enlightenment, Lady Shikibu must have felt newly inspired but equally dismayed that females in her time—and for many centuries after—were considered unable to attain the enlightened state.

Today, whether male or female, foreign or native, everyone is welcome at Engyoji—and whole heartedly. I didn't detect any lingering feelings that somehow females should not be able to visit this mountain top. Quite the contrary. After the passing of so many centuries these attitudes had happily been purged from this mountain sanctuary.

After arriving at the main temple compound, we climbed up the steep stone stairs to the hondo and upper temple complex, circled through the *Jikido*, or dining hall, where the movie *The Last Samurai* had been filmed, and, after completing our pilgrim rituals, looked for a suitable place to rest "the foot." The temple café beckoned with green tea and *yomogi mochi* (my favorite Japanese confection), a mugwort flavored glutinous rice glob surrounding a ball of sweetened red bean paste. (It might sound a bit disgusting, but I can assure you, it is not.) In fall, mochi are placed on outdoor grills which give them a warm and slightly chewy consistency that compliments the smooth interior.

The waitresses, true to the prevailing atmosphere, flitted around in a light cheerful mood. They too seemed happy and content, even though they probably had performed the same mundane kitchen/restaurant chores day after day, months on end. In their daily tasks they exuded a quiet sense of dignity and respect, and lacked any kind of haughty or bored "attitude."

After our afternoon refreshments, we headed over to the temple inn where we'd reserved a room for the night, along with special *shojin ryori* meals (special Buddhist-style vegetarian cuisine). The monk who greeted us at the front entrance, completely content, relaxed, and… happy, emanated a lightness that not all Buddhist monks possessed.

In our plastic slippers we shuffled behind him down a long smooth wood corridor, and then another one, struggling the whole time to keep our slippers from sliding off our feet. He laughed at our slipper difficulty and, before descending down a steep flight of narrow wooden stairs, suggested that we ditch the slippers. Which we did.

Our room, a traditional tatami mat room with sliding shoji doors and a verandah, overlooked a garden—mostly a view of the back of the temple inn, a kind of disheveled afterthought. Old weathered bamboo fencing, a few nandina, some maples, ferns and green nylon netting to protect plants from deer browse (I surmised), made up the majority of the landscape. A ladder or trellis lay sideways against a wood and stucco wall. A gate with a ceramic tile roof could be seen to one side. On the wooden verandah of our room, down at the end where you might not notice if you failed to poke your head around the corner, stood an old 48-inch flat screen TV (presumably broken). In our room, what would have been a traditional *tokanoma*, with poetic scroll and flower arrangement, now contained yet another flat screen TV (presumably not broken). We didn't turn it on, and felt disappointed that some temples (and this one in particular) had begun to cater to the needs of "tourist" pilgrims.

We had three hours before dinner and one book between us: *Mountain Tasting* by Santoka Teneda, a book of Zen haiku. Under the circumstances, it seemed apropos to read aloud. I noted a couple of my favorites:

Each day we meet
Both demons and Buddhas

The breeze from the mountains
In the wind bell
Makes me want to live

As the autumn sun moved into the afternoon low position, the room grew cold. We put on the wool kimono jackets that went with our cotton *yukatas* (light weight kimonos worn to and from the bath) and turned on the heater. Before long we were too hot; we turned it off. Hot or cold seemed to be the two options in Japan. I routinely either added a layer or took one off. But Santoka set me straight:

Is there anything I lack?
The leaves fall

In my journal I recorded two new words that day: *omi-e*, which is the picture prayer card of Kannon unique to each temple on the Kannon pilgrimage; and *yomogi*, mugwort—the green rice gluten part of the mochi.

A little writing, a little reading, a day of meandering around an ancient mountain top temple in autumn—indeed, we lacked nothing. And then it was mealtime.

Traditionally prepared, shojin ryori cuisine represents five colors, five tastes, and five textures. Purple, green, white, brown and orange enhanced and complimented rough, creamy, crunchy, smooth, and chewy, along with salty, sweet, bitter, sour and spicy—twelve delicious dishes.

A hot bath in the *ofuro* (honorable bath) after dinner and before bedtime is the usual custom. Because we hadn't paid attention to the kanji, we walked into the men's bath. Even though empty, we sensed something a miss. We walked out. Just then a woman came out of another door and complained about the bath water being too hot. Ah, then we saw the kanji for "woman" outside the bath door, and giggled over our mistake.

Luckily the large pilgrim group, still at dinner, left the bath empty except for us. But the scalding water, as we'd been warned, left us feeling cooked rather than relaxed. Still it warmed us for the long cold walk back to our room, seemingly a mile from either bath or bathroom.

Gwen would comment later:

autumn chill
the heated toilet seat
at the end of the hallway

Right before crawling into our cozy beds, I noticed something else crawling—a small red centipede making its way along the wall. Gwen directed it onto her document folder and moved toward the outside sliding door. It wouldn't open. I turned and twisted the knob, pulled and pushed at the door, but it wouldn't budge. In the scramble to rid our room of the centipede, it fell somewhere on our verandah, or on Gwen; we weren't sure. She brushed her clothes and shook them out, but we never saw the centipede again. The problem with uncertainty is that it fuels imagination, and mine conjured the red centipede crawling into my bed in the middle of the night.

Coupled with the loud snoring man above us, the thin paper walls, and the pillow that felt like a hard bag of rice (which it was), I popped a sleeping pill and called it a night. Before long it was time to attend the 6:30 chanting service with the monks.

Still groggy, and with a slight headache from a stiff neck, I got dressed and went to the front entrance to wait for everyone to gather. Even at that hour the other visitors seemed cheerful. The happy monk escorted us and the other group to the *Maniden Hall*, where the main deities are enshrined high up on the hill.

After the chanting service and a long dharma talk in Japanese, we went back to our inn for a shojin ryori breakfast of rice, miso soup, vegetables, pickled cucumber and tofu dishes. I thought of Santoka's poetic observation:

> *The warmth of the food*
> *Passes from hand to hand*

After breakfast we said goodbye to the happy cooks, the lighthearted monks, and all the other well-adjusted sentient beings on Mt. Shosha and headed for the cable car station along the old pilgrim route. On the way down I looked out over Himeji, now a modern city of half a million, and thought again about the devastation Japan suffered during World War II. The U.S. Military Command dropped 767 tons of incendiary bombs on Himeji, destroying over 60% of the inhabited area. Himeji Castle, also known as White Heron Castle because of its brilliant white walls and soaring architecture that resembles a bird taking flight, somehow survived the maelstrom. Some think the castle is divinely protected.

The cable car trip, languid and flawless, brought us back to the lower world of mundane affairs. But even here the day proceeded at a perfect pace. The bus going back to Himeji station arrived shortly after our descent. Everything per usual felt perfectly timed. And Santoka left me with:

> *Fallen leaves —*
> *Deep in the forest*
> *I see a Buddha*

Chapter 29

The sound of the waves
The rustling of the pines
A breeze from Nariai
Blowing across
The Bridge to Heaven

Nariaiji – Temple 28

A Glimpse of the Pure Land

From our train window many small hamlets, some with homes built in the traditional "praying hands" architectural style, and autumn colors in the surrounding hills complimented the gray branches of persimmon trees still lush with round orange fruit ready to be picked. Smoke from burning farm debris wafted across hillsides thick with timber bamboo. In the larger towns, purple-blue morning glories hung from apartment balconies. The ubiquitous power lines marred the otherwise pristine mountain landscape of cedar, fir and pine.

The cityscapes of Osaka and Kyoto had long been left behind as we headed toward the Japan Sea, and Amanohashidate, a famous area known as one of the three most scenic areas in all of Japan. Temple 28, Nariaji, our final destination, promised rare beauty.

Once we arrived, a map and a series of complicated instructions directed us through the village to the edge of a lagoon. There we caught a water taxi to the far shore. From the boat dock we crossed a busy street and followed the sidewalk upto and through the compound of a Shinto shrine. The path meandered around the back of the shrine and ended under the giant pillars of a cable car station. We boarded the cable car and rode up to the top of Mt. Nariasisen. Here we paused to

165

take in the spectacular view of sea, mountains and the Bridge to Heaven: a strip of undulating land with white sand beaches that connected two land masses. With barely a moment to take a photo, we quickly hopped on a bus that took us up a narrow one-lane twisting mountain road with gut tightening drop offs. At the Niomon the driver stopped to ask if we wanted to walk the rest of the way or take the bus. Even though I knew my foot wouldn't like it, we opted for walking.

The cable car and bus had accomplished the hard part. Now with ease we arrived at a five-story vermillion pagoda with relics of Buddha Shakyamuni embedded within. A shrine to Benzaiten complete with glassy tranquil pond lay off to the right. A flight of steep stone stairs took us to the Main Hall and central temple compound where every autumn color blazed under the cloud filled sky. Another lofty Pure Land on earth, Nariaji was a truly stunning mountain top temple far away in a remote part of Japan. But even here in this serene place of unparalleled natural beauty, the grating sound of civilization intruded into the quietude; this time a pressure washer at the end of a long blue hose that writhed like a giant snake across our path and nearly tripped me.

At Engyoji we'd had the smell of gasoline fumes from a leaf blower; at Ichijoji, the sound of a backhoe repairing typhoon damage; at Yoshiminidera, two leaf blowers. But more irritating than irritating sounds, my foot throbbed. I rubbed the healing vajra and mala in the hondo more than once and requested that all my hindrances be purified. I recited the Heart Sutra, and repeated 108 mantras. But in addition to mechanical noises, human noise began to encroach into my silent prayer. A group of loud foreign tourists arrived. Their piercing voices and laughter inserted themselves into my concentration. My rituals began to feel hollow and worthless. My peaceful state of mind began to erode.

Even in a Pure Land it's difficult to stay focused on one's purpose, to maintain a quiet mind.

Yet, I still felt blessed. Throughout our pilgrimage, a great deal of time was spent figuring out trains, buses, water taxis, cable cars and directions, and the other half in making sure we caught the last bus or the last cable car, or got on the right train on the right track and arrived at the right inn. Even so, true to any imagined Pure Land experience, we marveled that everything always fell into place. We would get off the train in a strange town, and there would be a man holding a sign for the inn that we had booked. With a smile and a nod, and a perfect welcome in English, he escorted us into his waiting van. How did he know to meet that particular train? Did someone arriving from another town on a different track call ahead? We would never know. We converged at the same time, at the same place, a perfect unfolding of synchronicity. Perhaps, whether we could see it or not, everything contained an order and purpose.

With all of our fumbling around in a foreign land, in a foreign tongue, we felt that someone or something was always looking out for us, helping, directing, and pointing the way. I've heard it said before by pilgrims, that the feeling of a benevolent hand, there to bless and guide their journey, felt ever present—so too on our Kannon pilgrimage, and so too at Nariaiji. Whatever arose as an obstacle in our mind's view, never materialized.

In some uncanny ways, Nariaiji felt consecrated by the hand of compassion reaching down from above. The tangle of transportation modes, although complex, unfolded seamlessly; the natural wonders unparalleled. Noisy pressure washer aside, this was a Pure Land of ease, a place of great beauty where one could get a glimpse of a realm (a state of mind you could say) where one might experience nirvana.

In Shin Buddhism, the Pure Land is a place (not necessarily an external place) presided over by Amida Buddha, (*Amitahba* in Sanskrit) the Buddha of Immeasurable Light. All deities are said to have their Pure Lands, a place where spirit (or consciousness) resides after leaving the body. These are special "in between" worlds where one is free of suffering and the round of negative karma, but still growing, still learning, still in training to realize even deeper layers of wisdom and compassion. Once achieved it is said that you can stay in the Pure Land or return as a bodhisattva to help other sentient beings. A Pure Land is a place that is physically lovely and perfect in every way. Nariaiji, despite the blue hose and noisy tourists, lingered in my mind as that kind of place, a physical manifestation of a state of mind right here in the earthly realm.

On the way back to the cable car, what had been a very calm day suddenly became breezy; then wind came whirling up from the sea. A rain cloud that hovered over the mountain appeared threatening. Without warning, rain came pouring out of the heavens and pelted the asphalt, the viewing platform and the cable car station. Akin to an Old Testament image where God blazes down through the firmament and commands his followers, I nearly expected to hear a voice or have a vision. The sudden downpour heightened the feeling of Nariaiji's special gift. An opening in the dark clouds allowed the sun to funnel through, creating an eerie light. Under cover of an umbrella that nearly twisted out of my hand by the ferocious wind, I somehow managed to take a few quick photos. Later on when I examined my images what had been captured gave me pause.

High in the sky, above the mountain, the sea, the temple and everything below, the sun shown through in the shape of a head, and below the head two giant arms of light stretched across the sky, and below the arms (dare I say, like a robe), light beams radiated down through the sky to the luminous sea right above the Bridge to Heaven, that infamous land bridge connecting heaven with earth. I could see what looked to be the outline of a giant sky being made of light.

No sooner had the rain and wind arrived out of nowhere than the air became calm, the storm shower passed, and the darkness lifted. We boarded the cable car with our dripping umbrellas and descended down the mountain to rejoin ordinary earthly existence.

Our experience at the top of the mountain, an experience that lasted an hour or two at the most, remained a dream like image of haunting beauty mixed with the power of earth's elements and the unseen spiritual forces seemingly at work all around us — perhaps a true "bridge to heaven," a portal to the extraordinary unlimited nature of reality? One could certainly be tempted to assign such a lofty evaluation to this sacred place.

Chapter 30

Since ancient times
How many lifetimes have passed?
For over a thousand years
At least I can depend
Upon Matsuno-o Temple

Matsuno-odera – Temple 29

The Real Buddhist

We arrived with instructions to look for the taxi office outside of the train station somewhere near the police station, but no sooner had we disembarked when a woman in casual business attire approached and said, "*Stamm-san desu ka?*" Before long we were off in our taxi headed for Temple 29.

Neither the woman nor the taxi driver understood why we wanted to see an old temple on a forgotten mountain road, when—we would discover much later—we could visit a more beautiful temple with gorgeous fall color right up the road. Not understanding about the "other" temple, and to appease the situation, we asked if the taxi driver could show us the historical Matsuno Train Station that some wanted torn down and others wanted to preserve.

Once we arrived at the deserted-looking train station, a calico cat, presumably homeless, and the only life left at the station, gave our taxi driver an opportunity to exercise his secret bodhisattva nature. He got out of his car with a bag of cat food and filled the bowl that someone had left inside. We walked around and pretended to admire the old historical station, but what remains in my mind even today is still the simple act of the taxi driver feeding an old forgotten cat.

Afterward, we headed for Temple 29 down a narrow road

that eventually ended at a turn-around with no other cars or great sights in view. Our driver would wait for an hour while we paid homage to Kannon.

Matsuno-odera, the most remote of our pilgrimage temples thus far had a feeling of being forgotten, but at the same time imbued with an immediate "good vibe": friendly and inviting. A sparkly older man sweeping leaves in knit cap, work boots and a ratty down jacket offered a warm and humble greeting. Using our favorite garden tool—a bamboo broom—he stopped to point out the 900-year-old gingko tree with an air of pride. We found some of its golden leaves and pressed them in a book. He so wanted to tell us about the temple, but with his limited English and our limited Japanese, the conversation remained, well, limited. Not until later, in a very rare moment when I felt inspired to have my picture taken with another human being— and after he took off his work jacket and cap to reveal a monk's indigo *samue* and shaved head—that I realized he was the head monk, casually doing the chores of an ordinary ground's keeper.

Way out in the middle of nowhere, a perfect place to contemplate and practice the teachings of Buddha, the monk felt like the "real deal," not a man who had to assume a temple in the family line (although he may have), not a monk who had to cater to the throngs of tourists and pilgrims that came to see some glorious, rare, site, but an ordinary monk who found the middle of nowhere to be the best place to be. True to the teachings of Buddhism, he represented a person who embodied the qualities of humility, generosity and compassion. Even without a common language, the monk's gestures, countenance, a look in his eye—the body communicates what is deep inside— spoke of something rare.

As far as extensive sub-temples, fabulous gardens or ancient pagodas, Matsuno-odera didn't offer much, but in terms of ambience, simplicity, humility and a kind of wild, ancient, other-worldly feeling, a time in the past when true Buddhism flourished, it won the prize. Even the Jizo statues with their extra faded bibs and faces of bliss peered out from under layers of tattered cloth with a special warmth.

Humility; that very un-American quality of inner quietude—of an unassuming nature devoid of show or arrogance, or boasting, bragging, self-important posturing, or anything resembling ego enhancement—permeated Matsuno-odera. An invisible bow of gratitude, of acknowledging the inner spirit that needs nothing from anyone, nor desires anything for itself, graced this quiet out of the way place.

Like the 900-year-old gingko tree that stood in one spot and silently watched the centuries go by, in another 900 years I hoped that this tree and temple and the humble spirit of the mountain would still be here—somewhat forgotten and neglected, like now, but still radiating the same light, only with a different set of leaves, a different monk sweeping them up. And the goeika echoes, "Since ancient times, how many lifetimes have passed?"

Perhaps it's best to be unknown and plain, a serene *wabi* kind of place where everything fades on the outside, but glows inwardly. The bibs on the jizos, the thick moss on the temizuya basin—a large hollowed out stone with ferns growing in the cracks—the tangle of falling timber bamboo that would eventually lay down on the forest floor, decay, and make good soil for new shoots, all conveyed a timeless presence. The wind of winter and time would blow through the mountain and change the forms, but not the formless, in that the spirit would remain—unassuming, barely noticeable, not important on anyone's tourist circuit, just an old rather lonely, yet lovely, and rustic place, an old monk sweeping leaves, smiling, offering a welcome hand, being gracious and leaving an indelible mark on one's spirit.

While we toured the temple grounds, a troop of young healthy men in blue uniforms arrived. They looked like the Japanese version of the National Guard. Were they at Matsuno-odera to clean up typhoon damage? To shore up a crumbling wall? Their attitude and disposition—congenial, energetic, self-disciplined—lent to the good-natured atmosphere. The leader explained a project, and in an orderly self-directed fashion the men disappeared behind one of the sub-temples to dutifully, even cheerfully, complete their work. They embodied an ingenuous integrity I'd witnessed before in the Japanese, perhaps a Zen quality encoded into their DNA.

We turned our attention toward a trail behind the hondo that led to a look-out point where, according to our pilgrimage information, a rope allowed you to pull yourself up to see the view. We walked a little way to get a feel for the ascent, but mostly to see the bamboo forest badly damaged by strong winds. Bamboo lay every which way, arched and tormented. With my injured foot and the taxi waiting we wouldn't be able to hike to the top, and anyway the twisted forest under a gray sky felt rather foreboding and uninviting. We turned around and went back to the temple office to get our pilgrim stamp, or nokyocho. The abbot wanted to know where we were from and how did we know about the Kannon pilgrimage. He said more foreigners were visiting his temple and he didn't know why.

We didn't say it, because it was impossible to properly translate to the abbot, but we both felt privileged to have experienced this remote temple on our pilgrimage route, and happy that at the end of our trip, Matsuno-odera was the final impression of our Part II finale. Even our ride back to the station proved to be blessed by yet another act of kindness: the taxi driver took it upon himself to drive us by the "other" temple. In the distance, we saw a magnificent pagoda against the stunning backdrop of autumn color, no doubt only one small aspect of this temple compound's treasures.

* * *

On the long train ride back to Kyoto I reflected on the experience of Temple 29, and the other temples on this leg of the journey. My foot pain and all its accompanying worries had not stopped me. I had kept the faith that somehow I would complete this pilgrimage and not give in to fear and anxiety. My new found determination and ability to face obstacles, to stare down worry, breathe fire on fear, to offer up suffering on behalf of others: these were all the gifts of my foot injury on pilgrimage. I felt a glimmer of satisfaction.

When we returned to Kyoto, an e-mail from a dharma organization wishing to form a Maha Sangha, or greater community of Buddhist practitioners, felt like a sign that people *did* want a more universal community; it reinforced the prayer I'd made throughout the pilgrimage that Buddhists and non-Buddhists (real and fakes) could awaken collectively, planetarily. A universal leap of consciousness seemed like the only hope we had of preserving our beautiful earth, and realizing the vision of a true democracy. All of us in our various roles—the monk in his work clothes, the temple waitresses serving tea and mochi, the men with the leaf blowers, the taxi driver with cat food, the "real" Buddhist, the pilgrims—had parts to play in awakening the heart of compassion. In ancient Sanskrit the word *sarvidaya*, "uplift for all," a word that Gandhi used for his political philosophy, captured the mood. Another translation, "everybody wakes up together," said it even better.

A sense of optimism and a belief that an ancient path traveled by millions had a magnifying power of its own—timeless and true—played in my thoughts at the end of our first pilgrimage trip. What lie ahead—the unfolding of events between the Ah and the Un—felt both exciting and terrifying in turn.

Epilogue

The relentless plantar fasciitus that plagued me for the entire second part of our pilgrimage imparted the lesson of determination and Right Effort. Not as dramatic as Bodhidharma cutting off his eyelids, it remained my own little statement that said yes, I'm serious, even with pain and fear and self-doubt, I am going forward on this journey to explore and celebrate the True Self, my inner Kannon. That's what this pilgrimage had become—an affirmation of life, of discovery, and an acknowledgement of the bodhisattva mind, the mind of wisdom and compassion. In essence, I was saying that I too will overcome what I must. And my foot was saying, okay prove it; show me that you mean business.

If there is pain, I choose to feel it.
Being with what is, I respond to what is.

Pilgrims had been confronting obstacles to their sacred journeys for millennia—sickness, danger, even death. My own obstacles, a far cry from the perils that others had confronted, felt rather insignificant, but still relevant. I came with a sore foot and I left with a sore foot, but my determination had strengthened. I could stand up to the scary monsters of fear and anxiety and see them as ghosts who disappeared under the light of faith, a belief in a calling, a yearning, a confidence in being led by one's inner being to do or be something, to participate in something ancient and holy that millions had done in the past and millions more would do in the future for as long as the steep stone stairs existed to be climbed. And what if all the temples could be reached someday by taxi, or bus or train—as many can now—then I say its an affirmation that we don't need to work and struggle and huff and puff our way to liberation anymore, but simply see the Truth for what it is—everything unfolding perfectly.

Part III

Preface

Between Part II and III of our pilgrimage, Gwen and I discovered and began to delve into biofield therapies, or energetic healing modalities: first in the form of Therapeutic Touch and eventually Reiki, as taught and practiced in Japan at the turn of the 20th century. A Buddhist priest named Mikao Usui developed techniques for spiritual attainment and healing around the early 1900s; what he discovered would later be known as Reiki. Often translated as "spiritual or life energy," Reiki has also been described by Frans Stiene in *The Inner Heart of Reiki* as "True Self," in essence our awakened mind, or Buddha-nature. Another way of describing our fundamental nature is found in this line from *Zazen Wasan, Song of Zazen* by Shodo Harada Roshi:

The universe is surging with this bright pure unattached essence, and we have never separated from it.

Our perceived "detour" into energetic healing, caught us both by surprise, and at first seemed a bit off course, but more and more I began to see it as a logical outcome of our pilgrimage of compassion. Inner Kannon directed us into more subtle states of awareness and led us to find ways to develop it; Reiki augmented our meditation practices and gave us a technique within the context of the Buddhist path to express that compassion. One of the five Reiki precepts states: Be Compassionate to Yourself and Others.

Reiki and other energetic healing techniques served to refine the inner senses, to help us connect consciously with a "higher" sense of self "never separated," and to forget or put aside concerns of the ego mind. Reiki directed us toward noticing, reflecting upon and eventually strengthening our inner world: an intangible, formless state of aware presence outside the bounds of self-centeredness that all the icons and symbols along the pilgrimage route pointed to. What could be more Kannon-like than that?

Reiki in Japan had been taught as a path to self-liberation and spiritual healing, in essence the foundation for all healing. To heal is to make whole, and wasn't that ultimately what we wanted for ourselves and the world? To be complete, inclusive and welcoming? To manifest equality and liberty for all?

When I reflected on my pilgrimage experience thus far, I recollected that I had, at each temple, made prayers and petitions to a representative of compassion. I had requested Kannon to lead me to an understanding of my essence; to manifest the dharma in my daily life; to bless and heal friends, family and strangers; and to bring peace to the world. I left nothing off my wish list and asked for the highest and best. Now I was being shown a tangible way to bring forth my own compassion and convey it to others. Had this mysterious endeavor called "pilgrimage," a journey into the heart of the divine feminine—Kannon—opened a gateway or portal into a whole new way of interacting with people, animals and the environment?

Following on the coat-tails of the 17th Karmapa's visit to Seattle that summer, "compassion" became the operative word—or I should say "compassion in action." The Karmapa emphasized that it was time to take compassion into the streets, so to speak, and to stop talking about it. The world needed "healing" on so many levels.

"Heal," a word on a lot of people's minds these days—how to heal our past, the earth, and the great divide among nations and people—meant how to ensure that love triumphed over hate, how wisdom won over ignorance, how compassion expressed itself as a strength rather than a weakness.

What began in 2012, the Year of the Dragon, as an exploration into the power of pilgrimage, the divine feminine, and the decade of my sixties, had now evolved into the new frontier of "healing"; it happened so gradually and unobtrusively that in the beginning I hadn't made the connection between it and our Kannon pilgrimage. But the obvious truth of it could not be ignored—the act of going on pilgrimage to 33 holy sites dedicated to the Buddha of Compassion; plus making prayers and supplications for awakening, had brought forth this new avenue of expression that facilitated the expansion of my potential. Compassion now had a tangible way to be developed, which in turn facilitated awakening. This was "skillful means" in process; this was the power of Kannon.

Chapter 31

Moon and sun are
Reflected in the troughs of the waves
At Chikubu Island —
Fill your boat here
With Kannon's treasure

Hogonji – Temple 30

Island of the Divine Feminine

Goldenrod and Japanese silver grass filled the wild areas along the train track as we made our way to Temple 30. *Susuki*, one of the Seven Grasses of Autumn, and used as a design motif on picture scrolls, lacquer ware, ceramics, folding screens, textiles and woodblock prints, became immortalized during the Heian Period and the Tale of Genji. Grasses, along with other wild plants, represented *mono no* aware, the poetic melancholy associated with impermanence and changing seasons. Silver grass (*Miscanthus sinensis*), revered in Japan, is offered to the moon during moon-harvest festivals.

Cultivated rice farms and vegetable gardens of mustard greens, sweet potatoes, peppers, carrots and daikon—the ubiquitous white radish that's pickled or eaten in autumn stews and soups—created a lazy quilt pattern of green textures across the countryside. The sun-sparkled waters of Lake Biwa, spread before a backdrop of purple-blue mountains, completed the picture of rural Japan that I loved—simple and rustic yet rich with symbolic seasonal imagery that poets and artists have drawn on since ancient times.

Our first temple on this, our last pilgrimage installment, had been built in 724 AD on Chikubushima (Bamboo Grove Island), a small islet in the middle of Lake Biwa, a freshwater lake thought to be over 4 million years old. In the *engi*, or sacred history of Chikubushima, a deity appeared to the monk Gyoki and said that this bit of lava rock with pine, bamboo and cryptomeria was born from a volcanic eruption and emerged overnight from "the Golden Layer," a Buddhist reference to one of the three layers beneath the earth. The deity went on to say that the island was a "Diamond Treasure Seat Rock where enlightenment may be reached." In ancient lore, the white cliffs rising above the lake expose the upper sheath of this sacred jewel.

Lake Biwa, sometimes called *Biwako*, refers to the shape of a stringed instrument. In the 14th century, a monk named Koso wrote that, "The lake is a Pure Land of the goddess Benzaiten because she lives on Chikubu Island and the shape of the lake is similar to that of the *biwa*, her favorite instrument."

Once a perilous journey for pilgrims in past centuries, our guidebook said that even today the trip by water taxi could be a bit rough. But on our day in October, a sunny day with clear skies and a predicted temperature of 76 degrees, we didn't anticipate any challenges. The morning after we arrived in Japan, jet-lagged and still a little headachy from our fifteen-hour flight, we set off at 7:30 AM for Kyoto Station, about 45 minutes by bus from our inn.

Before our departure, a Japanese friend confirmed that a boat from Omi Imazu on the west side of Lake Biwa was a better option than Nagahama on the east side of the lake. A Special Rapid from Kyoto Station would take us directly to the port in 50 minutes.

As our train continued its route along the shores of this historically rich body of water—the largest freshwater lake in Japan—expansive collections of solar panels inserted themselves into the golden rod, grass plumes and farmscapes. On this trip we saw more and more solar farms, and learned later that ever since the Fukushima nuclear disaster of 2011, solar energy has boomed in the Land of the Rising Sun. The Japanese have even begun converting abandoned golf courses into mega-solar farms.

Once we arrived at Omi Imazu, thoughts of alternative energy gave way to thoughts of finding our way to the harbor. Our guidebook mentioned taking a taxi, but the taxi driver pointed toward the lake and said we could walk.

Within five minutes we'd found the little ticket office and shop in front of a long boat dock. Round-trip tickets in hand, we sat on a bench overlooking the lake like two expectant children and ate our bento lunch. Only four boats per day made the trip. A forty-minute wait gave us plenty of time to finish lunch and ruminate over a pair of pilgrim sandals in the tourist shop. The sandals, made out of old rags and dyed in bright colors, harkened back to days gone by when pilgrims wore straw sandals and a conical hat, carried a staff, and donned white clothing—white symbolizing death and impermanence in Japan. The sandals represented the humble nature of pilgrimage and the prevailing thought that to perish while walking the pilgrim's path bestowed a blessing. We bought both pairs and settled back down on our bench to gaze at the lake.

The beautiful sunny day promised to offer a mild and carefree crossing, and I felt a surge of excitement and wonder at the prospects of experiencing such an ancient holy place. Who would have dreamed a thousand years ago, when pilgrims, monks and emperors traveled by wooden boat, that we in the 21st century (foreign pilgrims at that, and women) would still be crossing these waters to experience the essence of the Divine Feminine. Now we journeyed in shiny aluminum and fiberglass motor boats with air-conditioning and vending machines. Our technology had changed, but had our yearning?

SacredJapan.com per usual provided the deepest and most spiritual outlook on Chikubushima. Kodo explained how, "this mystical island is steeped in legends and folklore, and its caves were home to many hermits, shamans and wandering monks dating back into the mists of time." Coupled with three female

Shinto deities appropriated into the Buddhist story as Benzaiten and Kannon, "the island's main energy seems to be the Divine Feminine itself."

By the time the boat arrived for the trip, a feeling of expectancy mixed with awe and wonder washed over me. Only a few other visitors took the trip with us. I had expected a bigger crowd for a place steeped in centuries of history and lore, but glad not to be part of a mob scene the likes of Kiyomizudera, Temple 16.

We sat under an awning on the top deck where the breeze and views were best and looked toward the small speck in the distance. Everyone on the boat maintained quiet, courteous and expectant behavior. Conversations carried on in low tones; photo taking was discreet.

As we grew closer, the speck turned into a large rock with greenery, and then a small mountain with steep tan cliffs and bamboo forests. As we rounded a corner, the cliffs gave way to a harbor, docks and a set of steep stone stairs that brought the eye to rest upon a vermillion pagoda at the top of a small mountain. No one lives on Chikubushima, but every day temple stewards, and vendors for the few souvenir shops, travel to the island to serve the public and pilgrims.

Our boat docked and everyone filed out to greet the day. Once we left the row of souvenir shops along the harbor, the climb zigzagged up the hill, and the special energy of this sacred place began to well up in me. Since studying and practicing healing systems my intuitive faculties had sharpened. I "sensed" more. Without a doubt this island was a special place beyond description.

Up and up we went with all the other people from our boat until we reached the hondo and Bentendo. Inside, two striking wooden images of Benzaiten, the goddess of music, poetry and all that flows, stood in opposite corners. No Buddha Shakyamuni here, only tributes to the Divine Feminine. And yet had women traveled here in centuries past? Had Chikubushima, like so many other sacred places in Japan, been off limits to women until the 20th century?

According to the Noh play, *Chikubushima*, an old fisherman and a young woman are solicited by a court official to take him and his entourage to the island. At first the old man objects, saying that this is a fishing boat not a ferry. But when the official says that he is making his first pilgrimage to Chikubushima, the old man says, "indeed this is a holy place... one should not trifle with the gods."

Once they reach the other shore, the old man says, "You see here the Celestial Goddess Benzaiten. Please pray as your heart moves you to do."

The nobleman turns to the young woman and says, "They say this place is forbidden to women. Why is a woman with us before the shrine?"

The old man replies, "Your question betrays your ignorance. This goddess, awesome to tell, is an incarnation of eternal enlightenment; therefore women are particularly welcome at her shrine."

The chorus chimes in:

Benzaiten has a woman's form;
Benzaiten has a woman's form;
and her divine power is truly wondrous.
Since she appears as a Celestial Lady,
she and all women are really one....

Later in the story, the young woman transforms into Benzaiten and disappears into the shrine. The old man reveals himself to be the Dragon God of Lake Biwa and plunges into the depths. Thus the story imparts a lesson to the noble on the nature of reality, the joining of above and below into a unity of wholeness.

That said, the history of Chikubushima is filled with stories of only male Buddhist masters who left their imprint on this island. Kobo Daishi, founder of Shingon Buddhism; Dengyo Daishi, the founder of Tendai Buddhism; Jikaku Daishi, a famous Tendai priest; and En no Gyojo, the founder of Shugendo, are all thought to have spent time on this island. Many other seekers of Truth journeyed to Chikubushima, including famous warlords, as well as unknown wandering monks. All of them had, in one way or another, made their way to this dot in the middle of Lake Biwa to perform Buddhist rituals and austerities, to meditate, pray and absorb the feminine energy of this rock which En no Gyojo proclaimed to be that of Benzaiten. Even before Buddhism arrived in Japan, this island, considered a sacred Shinto site, bore archeological findings going back to the time of the Jomon Period, roughly around 12,000 BC.

Even without knowing the history of Chikubushima, one could feel the vibrational purity of this special place, an ancient site surrounded by pristine sparkling water, legends and mystery. Yet, as with so many other temple visits on our pilgrimage, limitations dictated by public transportation—this time by boat schedules (we had to return on the same boat that we arrived)—compelled us to make haste, only touching the surface of the magic of Hogonji. We barely had time for our temple rituals, let alone time to explore any of the off-the-beaten-track nooks and pathways, or stay still and quiet long enough to absorb some of the energized ions that certainly hovered in such a place. Rather, Chikubushima left me with a fleeting impression of an ancient place filled with unimaginable history and special exalted air, a blur of steep stone stairs, exquisite statuary, stunning views over glistening waters, an ancient tree held up with a lattice work of bamboo poles, vermillion torii gates and friendly temple priests. To stay for any length of time to absorb the depth of place was out of the question. And so we dutifully returned to our boat, after the allotted 75 minutes, still yearning for more, still wanting to let another layer of ancient sacred presence seep into our bones. I had to be satisfied with a holy picture card of Benzaiten and my temple stamp, more the acquisition of a tourist than a pilgrim, although I managed to recite the Heart Sutra, 108 mantras of *Om Mani Padme Hum*, and make a plea to remove obstacles to seeing my True Self, as I understood those words.

How does one absorb the stories and lingering imprints of a place traveled by spiritual wanderers and holy beings over the centuries? Perhaps it wasn't possible. Certainly not in a mere 75 minutes of rushing through on a timeline.

The island felt so special, and our time there so brief, we contemplated going back at the end of the week. But would we? It was a long trip with a fair amount of expense, and so in the end the idea of going back was more wishful thinking than a practical reality.

What lingers in my memory, the imprints of form are these: two intricately carved statues of Benzaiten with enigmatic Noh-like smiles (the oldest Benzaiten statues in Japan); a large stone incense basin with mounds of soft ash and a few wisps of smoke wafting in the air; a steel case with flickering white candles; a wooden box where pilgrims piled copies of their calligraphic tracings of the Heart Sutra and one opposite where I placed my petition: "May we all awaken in this life."

And if I went back, what would I be looking for, or hoping to find? How could I touch the heart of this place and all who had come before me? This speck of an island, a mere 1.2 miles in circumference had intrigued and compelled seekers of spirit to travel the waters of Lake Biwa for thousands of years to experience its flavor and feeling. Islands did that—they enticed. Surrounded by water, small islands, cozy and safe, felt removed from the fray as if one had found a raft in the middle of the great mother's fluid body. Islands, a symbol for our own bodies, represented a lump of matter suspended in a sea of divine consciousness yet never apart from it. Were Kannon and Benzaiten *there* anymore or less than they were *here*? Weren't we the Celestial Goddess wherever we went? Maybe on an island in the middle of a lake it was easier to feel that presence; and wasn't it that remembrance, our own divine nature, that we yearned for?

On the way back to the mainland, the ferry operator played a song over the loud speakers. The Japanese seemed very familiar with it as one woman sang along under her breath. I couldn't be sure what she was singing, but suspected that it might be the goeika for Hogonji. The words "fill your boat here with Kannon's treasure," captured the flavor of our visit. We sought to reveal our compassionate heart, and aspired to fill our lives and world with happiness and contentment. On Chikubushima, I'd had an ever so brief taste of "filling my boat" with the essence of Kannon. I felt like singing too.

Chapter 32

May you live for 8,000 years
Oh willow of Chomeiji,
Temple of long life —
Let us carry you in our hearts
As we go on our journey

Chomeiji – Temple 31

Stairway to Heaven

The over-riding thought, before and after our visit to Chomeiji, remained the 808 steps—very steep stone steps—leading to the top of Mt. Ikiya, the home of Chomeiji since 836 AD. The equivalent of a 57-storey building, our pilgrim book described the steps to Chomeiji as "...very slick, rough and uneven..." That first phrase, "very slick" nearly stopped us. I imagined slipping and plummeting headfirst into an abyss.

But, as with many other anxieties that arose during pilgrimage, I had learned to let that thought go by like a passing cloud, and vowed instead to ascend the 808 steps and dedicate the merit to those who were ill or distressed back home. Everyone it seemed suffered from either a physical, mental or spiritual dis-ease, so in essence I dedicated my walk to all sentient beings.

Fortified with a purposeful intention, the day unfolded under beautiful sunny skies and warm temperatures—a typical October day in Japan that made for easy hiking. Once we located the stairs across from the bus stop that led to Chomeiji, we took a deep breath, a drink of water, and began our ascent. For at least the first ten minutes we were the only two pilgrims on the stairs; then a woman in her 30s came bounding down; later a young couple passed us going up. Other than these three people, and an elderly gentleman near the top, we had the 808 steps to ourselves. The stairs, not slick per our guidebook warning, were very rough, uneven, and steep, a typical hand-built staircase of old stones embedded into the side of the mountain one rock at a time. I let the ancient steps take me to that timeless place when pilgrims still wore straw sandals and carried a staff. How many feet had trodden up the mountain on these stones? How many minds had turned away from the mundane world to enter the realm of the deities?

We soon entered a bamboo forest. Twisted, fallen and broken timber bamboo lie strewn this way and that as though a wrathful wind had blown through without a care for what lay in its path. Stately cryptomeria had fared better; their thick trunks withstanding the onslaughts of time and weather—and turbulent winds—but still shedding branches along the way. An unkempt corridor of forest where few people traveled and fewer still tended, the steel hand rail that once ran up the middle to offer assistance to pilgrims, was long gone. Only the pole sockets could still be seen. Yet the stairs, old and majestic in their austerity, transported me back to the days of the ancient pilgrim's path before paved roads and shiny cars took the devoted to the top.

Chomeiji has a long history of healing, and indeed all along the way, the air felt charged with potential. I took my time, not only to catch my breath, but to absorb the timeless quality, the feeling of place, the beautiful scenery, and the knowledge that centuries of pilgrims had walked up and down this mountain path. When I began to worry about mastering the 808 steps, I counted them. Surprised at how quickly I knocked off 100, the stairs became a metaphor of mindfulness: stay focused on the present moment, don't look back; don't anticipate what lay ahead.

Quicker than expected, we reached the top. A beautiful little temple with hondo, pagoda and bell tower awaited us, along with dreamy views over Lake Biwa and the distant landscape.

We took in the view, found the bell tower, and took turns climbing the ladder, pulling back the massive log and letting it strike the giant bronze bell three times for Buddha, Dharma and Sangha. After sounding the bell, I sat outside the hondo to recite the Heart Sutra and mantra. With each *Gate Gate Paragate Parasamagate Bodhisvaha!* (Which means, Gone Gone, Gone Over, Gone Fully Over; Awakened! So be it.) I visualized someone I knew who was ill, depressed, stressed, grieving or suffering in some way. At Chomeiji my visualizations felt clear and sharp, more focused. Perhaps all the oxygen pumped into my brain from huffing and puffing to the top gave me renewed clarity, but I rather think the charged ions, or special energy, found at sacred sites radiated forth from the site itself—a geological wonder with mammoth boulders set into the mountain.

Chomeiji had been a sacred Shinto healing center since the time of Emperor Keiko around 71-130 AD. Five centuries later, after Buddhism established itself in Japan, Prince Shotoku, once thought to be an emanation of Kannon, declared that Kannon's healing power was intensified here. A vision instructed him to carve three images of Kannon from willow tree wood. In those days, a healing ritual entailed carving an image of a Buddha or bodhisattva to invoke a cure. In the case of Chomeiji an image of Kannon, carved for Empress Suiko, dispelled her illness. Chomeiji is thus known as the long life or longevity temple. Indeed, the atmosphere felt infused with something powerful, even though our pilgrim book said, "there is not much here." Yes, there are no fabulous gardens, exceptional statues, museums or sprawling temple grounds with ponds and koi as you might find at some other temples, but Chomeiji has—for lack of a better term—good vibes; it poured forth. I soaked up the sound of the bell, felt the energy radiating from the boulders and the intensity of sun that sparkled across Lake Biwa. The glittering water, the boulders, the air itself exuded prana, the life force of all healing; it brought clarity of mind and a peaceful feeling to my being.

After our rituals we walked around the upper grounds and looked down on the exquisite temple roof lines in the *irimoya* style, with wood beams and cypress thatch in the hip and gable design. One-hundred thousand thatched roof buildings still exist in Japan, and three hundred professional thatchers keep the craft alive despite declining cypress bark, the preferred thatching material. Something of the organic, earthy nature of thatched roofs felt pleasing to the spirit. Also very durable, they could last up to fifty years. The thatched temple roofs of Chomeiji, one aspect among many, made this a charming and uplifting place, a place that felt restorative, magical and powerful.

From anywhere on the grounds one could look out over Lake Biwa and the distant mountains. The steps of an upper level shrine became a quiet place to sit and eat a bento lunch without the distraction or disruption of other pilgrims. We absorbed as much as we could of the rarified air before reluctantly confronting our descent. The steps or the road? We chose the road to save on legs and avoid the potential for trips or spills.

Once we arrived at the bus stop, life returned to mundane matters: checking the bus schedule, watching a little boy chase after a stray cat. While we waited, I previewed my photos. I paused at the one showing the first glimpse of the 808 stairs. The rough stone steps rose up into the trees and disappeared into forest foliage as if something out of a mysterious dream; the staircase enticed, and dared one to make life's ascent into the unknown.

Chapter 33

Oh, precious One
Please guide us
Here at Kannon temple —
We have come from so far
On our journey

Kannonshoji – Temple 32

Lost in Kannon's Pure Land

The journey to Kannonshoji soon became one of spiritual wanderers lost in a foreign land while trying to find their way to the holy mountain top. Our guidebook said to take a bus from the train station to Kannonshoji-guchi and walk 2 kilometers. We did as instructed and walked toward the distant mountain sure to be our destination. We passed through a quiet neighborhood with gardens and persimmon trees, came upon a large old temple on the right side of the road and thought we had arrived, but nothing looked quite right—no people, temple offices, stewards, grounds keepers, pilgrims... The place was deserted. A Japanese couple came along and said this was a Shinto shrine. They didn't know anything about Kannonshoji. But together we found a sign that said Kannonshoji, 350 meters with an arrow that pointed further up the road. Relieved, we continued only to find another deserted temple, and another sign that said Kannonshoji, with distance and walking time and an arrow pointing up the mountain. The road soon turned into a path, and the path turned into steps that went up the mountain. We followed the path and the signs, and soon were ascending the steep stone stairs to another group of buildings. They too were deserted, but another sign enticed us to continue up the mountain. Undaunted, we tarried on, even though there were no other pilgrims on the path, only two bicycles that had been left at the base of the stairs, and another sign with meters and the time it would take to walk. Focused on reaching our second to last pilgrimage temple, up we went to a level area with benches and views overlooking the town and valley. Two older women (presumably the bicycle owners) sat on a bench eating lunch and talking. They didn't pay us any attention.

Another sign, Kannonshoji, 1,300 meters, 60 minutes, pointed up the mountain. Okay, that's way more than 2 kilometers. Not reaching Temple 32 was not an option, but should we continue on this path? Was the sign a mistake?

Determined but skeptical, we continued. The path, strewn with forest debris and draped in spider webs (and large spiders)—bigger spiders than I enjoyed seeing—gave us pause. The path kept going up and up through spider webs and downed tree limbs. I picked up a stick to clear away the webs and mumbled that there surely had to be another way to Kannonshoji. No one had walked this path in a long, long time, and no one had maintained it in years. A couple hundred meters up this primitive trail, not knowing where it would end, or where we were going, with no maps or other pilgrims to guide us, I said, "There has to be another way." Gwen hesitated. What if this was it? What if this was the only way to Kannonshoji?

No, there had to be another way. "We have to go back."

What if the last test of our perseverance remained this primitive, untraveled path up a dark and lonely mountain populated by "giant" spiders? Even though Gwen looked worried that somehow, so close to finishing our pilgrimage, we might not be able to find our second to last temple, she agreed, we had to go back. We returned to the area with the benches and the view where we'd seen the two women, presumably locals. Surely they would know the way to Kannonshoji.

Luckily they were still there deep in conversation. We asked them how to get to Kannonshoji, but they had never heard of it. One of the women, in typical Japanese style, got up to look around and be helpful. She spotted the sign: Kannonshoji, 1,300 meters, 60 minutes. Yes, we know, we said. Everyone looked perplexed. After a few more times going back to look at the sign, confirming that yes it said Kannonshoji, we thanked them, and discussed our options.

For a few moments we experienced something close to panic at the thought of not being able to finish our pilgrimage. At the same time, we were certain that there had to be another way. We'd have to walk down the mountain, back to the bus stop, wait for another bus, go back to the train station and ask a taxi driver if they took pilgrims to Kannonshoji. Almost all of the Kannon temples have an access road with taxi service. What if this was one of the exceptions?

An hour later, tired, cranky, a little worried, we arrived back at the train station and asked the first taxi driver we saw — a female, and a rarity in Japan — if she could take us to Kannonshoji. Yes, for 2,300 yen one-way (about $20), the taxi driver deity agreed to take us to Kannonshoji. Willing, at this point, to pay any price to reach Temple 32, we jumped into her car relieved, but still perplexed as to where this darn temple could be.

Our personal "Kannon" drove out of town and followed the same route as the bus. For a moment we thought we might end up back at the same place, only a little poorer. Then what? But at a fork in the road, our All Knowing One turned right instead of left, and we knew, yes, there was another way to Kannonshoji. Soon we were climbing a mountain on a one-lane windy road with death-defying switch backs. We came to a toll booth. Did we want to pay 600 yen for our taxi to pass through? Yes! We would have paid anything.

At the top of the mountain a barrier prevented cars from continuing beyond a small parking lot. Our taxi goddess would wait an hour as we continued by foot up the road to the temple. (The 2 kilometers?)

All along the 15-minute walk from the car park to the temple gate, we saw pathways leading down the mountain. Did one of them connect to the 1,300 meter, 60-minute path? Would it have eventually led to this road? SacredJapan.com did say something about "eight approach pathways up the mountain."

As we came around a bend in the road two magnificent Nio and one of the finest examples of Amida Buddha greeted our arrival. We stopped to admire Amdia Buddha's hands in the mudra of meditative equipoise. Calm washed over me. Further on, nestled high up on a mountain made of unusual rounded boulders, stood two ten-foot high Kannons, one with her vase of spiritual nectar and the other holding a lotus bud of Buddha potential. A lotus pond surrounded the base of the mountain like a protective moat. A bridge crossed over the lotus pond and ended at a Shinto shrine dedicated to the mountain kami, a thunder god. The power and magnificence of this mountain of boulders was unrivaled; like the boulders at Chomeiji, it emanated a force field of extraordinary vigor.

Inside the hondo, a large Thousand-armed Kannon carved out of wood filled the interior sanctuary with her presence. Not until you knelt down on the tatami mat in front of the main altar to make prayers, did you see the milky moon-like mirror at the level of Kannon's heart. Ah, is that why Kannon had a knowing smile?

An hour wasn't nearly enough time to take in this exceptional temple. When it came to pilgrimage temples the motto seemed to be "no lingering, no attachment." The few moments we had to savor the experience were precious and fleeting, the way Buddhists describe the nature of our existence.

I recited the Heart Sutra, mantras, the Kannon Sutra, and filled out my prayer slip with the request that we have compassion for all. I received my pilgrim stamp, lit a candle for my parents and three sticks of incense for Buddha, Dharma and Sangha, purified myself with the incense smoke, took photos and reluctantly walked back to the waiting taxi. I left behind my prayers, my reverence, and my delight. I took away Kannon's smile with my image at her heart.

Several months later, one of Gwen's former Japanese students looked into the mysterious route to Kannonshoji. She informed us that, yes, there are two paths (and perhaps more) up the mountain, a front and a back route, both of them beginning near where the bus had dropped us off, and both, per internet images looking primitive and rarely traveled. I chocked up our mountain adventure to Kannon's way of giving us one last little hurdle to overcome, one last doubt to transcend; one final fear to rise above. Take one step at a time with no thought, no expectation of certainty.

Chapter 34

Vows made here
For all times all worlds
At Tanigumi
Where the waters flow
From the moss

Because it is a sign
Of the Buddha
Who lights up the whole world,
The flame here
Has never gone out

The pilgrim cloaks
Relied upon until today
As a child relies on a parent—
We now take off and leave here
As offerings, at Tanigumi in Mino

Kegonji – Temple 33

The Taste of Sweet Persimmons

At 5:30 AM on the last day of our pilgrimage, I sat in my little convenience apartment in Kyoto drinking a pot of tea and wondering what the day would bring. An infinite number of events, adventures, mishaps and miracles potentially awaited us.

Over the course of the pilgrimage, I had watched my mind get hooked by so many fears and worries—thoughts that came and went like turbulent weather fronts. Each time I told myself to stay in the present moment, to focus on the step that I could see, feel, and touch.

I thought about the texture of those steps. The ones from centuries past—rough, uneven, irregular, organic and more aesthetically pleasing—contrasted with the steps built in modern times—smooth, even, and lacking in character. The modern steps—much like life in the 21st century—offered ease, uniformity and a hygienic sameness. I yearned for the ancient ones—authentic, heartfelt, and poetic.

Although the conveniences and gadgets of my generation had their merits, they didn't replace the beauty of the steep stone stairs that had been cut and laid, one by one, by individual hands and bodies grunting under the strain and weight and difficulty of placing all those irregular stones into impossibly steep slopes without the aid of modern equipment. The people from ancient times desired to build stairways to the gods, and they did. Through their hard labor and devotion they had assisted countless others to experience the glory of reaching summits of mind, body and spirit. Their effort, although to them probably small and insignificant at the time, carried forward for centuries. Would my own effort create benefit in ways I couldn't see or comprehend?

Many challenges emerged throughout the course of our pilgrimage: strenuous hikes and health concerns, uncertainty, doubt, fear and anxiety. The three trips to Japan, over a four-year period, had been exhilarating but physically exhausting, adventurous but also stressful. Would I do it again?

* * *

As our train traveled farther away from Kyoto and the morning rush hour, the crowds thinned. Seats opened up for the rest of the trip. We changed trains at Maibara and again at Ogaki where we had 5 minutes to find the train for Tanigumiguchi, a stop so remote that it wasn't listed on our train map.

At Ogaki we changed tracks, bought a separate ticket and

headed for a one-car train waiting for us to finish our transaction. Before long we were deep in farm country with rice fields yet to be harvested, tangerine groves and persimmon trees heavy with sweet fruit. As before, wild goldenrod plumes mixed with Japanese silver grass. Fields of pink, white and magenta cosmos completed the late October seasonal motif. Maple leaves had only barely begun to show color in the mountains. The ginkgos, usually a deep golden color in November, were still vibrant green.

Now, at the end of our journey, I felt a sense of relief coupled with sadness. My sister and I had shared something grand and adventurous together that we would cherish to the end of our days. We had traveled to parts of Japan that most foreigners never see. We had seen exquisite Buddhist art created by skillful hands, hands that had reverence and a deep feeling for the inner spiritual life that the statues served to remind. We had walked through beautiful gardens, admired unique architecture and marveled at ancient stone work. We had deepened our feeling and knowledge of Buddhism, and the spirit of Kannon. We had met wonderfully helpful Japanese, who had guided us, made phone calls for us, gave us directions and tips, and sometimes even walked the pilgrim's path with us. To these modern day bodhisattvas we would always be grateful. Most importantly, we had contemplated the compassionate life, been led to healing arts and opened ourselves to new inner worlds.

Now, here we were traveling yet another train to an unfamiliar destination, perhaps a route we would never return to, and to a place that had not seen many foreigners. When an elder woman on the train commented on my fair skin, I knew we were in deep Japan. That and the lack of young people on our train, indicated the distance from big cities with their offer of universities, entertainment and jobs.

Our one-car train, where everyone talked and laughed and exchanged stories, felt like a party train; it stood in stark contrast to the city trains where everyone looked down, slept, read the newspaper or fiddled with their smart phones. The one-car train from Ogaki to Tanigumiguchi took forty-one minutes and offered the best of human spirit, a feeling of celebration on our last pilgrimage journey.

We passed through more farms and hamlets before coming to a stop at perhaps the tiniest station in Japan—a wooden shed with a couple of benches next to the one track and one platform. The conductor called our stop, and we disembarked. With only five buses a day to Temple 33, we had arrived in time for the first one at 9:51 AM.

The bus driver looked well beyond retirement age. Did he *want* to keep working, or did he *have* to keep working. I wondered how many years he'd been transporting pilgrims from the train station to the final pilgrimage temple, the last stop. Maybe it was his own form of osetai, an offering made to those on pilgrimage.

Unlike Kannonshoji, the route to Temple 33, clear and direct, brought us to the beginning of a long tree-lined street with souvenir shops, antique stores, vegetable stands, tea houses and cafes. One could buy anything from radish roots to persimmons to expensive Kannon scrolls, incense, prayer beads or a bowl of matcha with a seasonal sweet. A large parking lot, mostly vacant on the day of our visit, indicated that big crowds of pilgrims and tourists frequented this temple—perhaps especially in spring when the whole avenue leading up to the temple would be awash with pink cherry blossoms, or in November when the temple compound would be aglow with red maples. From the billboards, we gathered that this hamlet also hosted a lily festival in summer, and special religious festivals throughout the various seasons. A unique place—the culmination of a very long pilgrimage of compassion—Kegonji inspired the contemplation of endings, of new beginnings, of joy and sadness, and the question, what would life be like back home post-pilgrimage?

Although neither of us remembered reading any rave

reviews of this temple, we found it to be exceptionally beautiful and appropriate to the Buddhist story. The grounds, filled with many icons, told various aspects of Buddha Shakyamuni's life story. Near the entrance, a baby white elephant reminded the viewer that Buddha's birth mother, Queen Mahamaya, dreamt of just such an elephant entering her womb through her side. Because elephants symbolized greatness in ancient Nepal, wise men of the day foretold that the Queen would thus give birth to a great being.

Across the stone walkway, and sitting in the lotus posture on top of a large boulder, Emaciated Buddha (not yet a Buddha) told the story of his extreme austerities before the milkmaid offered him sustenance. When her drink revived him, Buddha saw the error of extremes and proclaimed the Middle Way.

Further along the path a stone carving of Buddha in the reclining position had the unusual addition of a disciple (probably Ananda) standing behind him, along with two other disciples standing nearby in a grove of trees to bear witness to Buddha's physical passing.

Shinto foxes, messengers of the god/goddess Inari (associated with the Hindu goddess Dakini), stood as prominent icons among the Buddhist story. Inari looks after farms and farming, especially rice, a staple considered sacred in Japan. For some reason, Inari is often missing and instead replaced by his messengers, the magical shape-shifting fox protectors. The foxes also guard Shinto shrines against negative influences.

Jizo Bodhisattva appears in numerous forms: sometimes as a cute infant/child, sometimes as a stately looking monk, sometimes as an androgynous bodhisattva. Jizo, once Ksitigarbha, an Indian female deity who rescued her mother from the hell realms through her great merit, later became the male Jizo Bodhisattva. Kegonji, like many Buddhist temples throughout Japan, had various versions of this popular deity.

Nearer the temple, at the base of a set of stairs, twin bronze

Kannon's about 20 feet high, made an imposing welcome. One of the Kannons held her hands folded in prayer, and the other held a lotus bud, symbol of our Buddha potential.

After passing the twin Kannons, we climbed our last set of steep stone stairs that led up to the hondo, and the hillside in back. Here ropes and ropes of *senbazuru*, 1,000 origami cranes, hung from every rafter, gate and door, from every hook or beam—wherever one could find a spot, there hung another rope of colorful cranes. The cranes had been folded for health, longevity, truth, and most importantly for peace. They served to remind all who came to Kegonji of the horrors and tragedy of war, the innocent victims, and especially the young girl Sadako Sasaki who contracted leukemia after being exposed to the radiation of Hiroshima. She heard of the senbazuru legend that anyone who folded 1,000 cranes would be granted a wish. The ropes of cranes would always remind the world of the tragedy of atomic weaponry, and the wishes of those who sincerely prayed for world peace.

Inside the shrine alcove surrounded by cranes, priests had piled the standard white shirt and pants that pilgrims once wore, along with straw conical hats and wooden staffs. No longer gear of the modern Saigoku pilgrim, still these symbolic implements left a powerful impression of all who had come before throughout time. Thousands, perhaps millions of wanderers seeking healing of body, mind and spirit, those wishing for world peace, enlightenment or a life transformation of some kind, had all traveled through this temple. In a neighboring shrine, thousands of baby bibs with wishes written on them hung in row after row, and every conceivable wall space inside the shrine. A young couple with their infant strapped onto the front of the Dad arrived at the same time as our visit. They took the bib from around their baby's neck and placed it in among the others. Like thousands of parents before them, they came here to wish for a long and healthy life for their child, a wish that parents have in every corner of the world. These two shrines together, permeated with the heartfelt aspiration of love, peace, health and happiness—what everyone wanted for themselves and others, no matter what nationality, religion, sexual preference or race— echoed the dreams of humankind. We wanted to be happy, to realize our highest potential, to bask in the glorious sun ray of pure being without prejudice, judgment, hatred, envy, malice or anger.

After reveling in all that Kegonji had to offer, we reluctantly descended the steep stone stairs and took our time along the walkway that led out of the temple gate. We took in the Kannons, the Buddha Shakyamuni's, Buddha's disciples, the Jizo Bodhisattva's, the elephant, the Shinto foxes, Benzaiten with her lute, the Seven Lucky Gods, Fudo Myo'o and many other icons telling the Buddhist story. If we'd known at the time about the circumambulation route beneath the temple, we would have paid our final respects to Kannon by walking clockwise in total darkness around her image.

We continued along the promenade toward the shops and cafes, bought some incense, a couple of Kannon amulets and a cloth bowl made with indigo fabric. A woman at a fruit stand handed me a peeled persimmon in an attempt to sell me an entire basketful. I tasted the sweetness and offered to buy it, but she gave it as a gift.

Kosho Uchiyama's book *Opening the Hand of Thought* came to mind. He describes two kinds of persimmon trees—one sweet, one astringent—and says, "When you plant seeds from a sweet persimmon tree, all the saplings come up as astringent persimmon trees." How very strange. In order to produce a sweet persimmon tree you have to graft it to an astringent variety. He goes on to say that the persimmon tree is indigenous to Japan and has been around for thousands of years. To get that first sweet fruit from a persimmon tree, the tree must be 100 years old.

The analogy of the sweet persimmon describes Buddha Shakyamuni as the sweet fruit that ripened among the astringent quality of humanity. The branches of Buddhism, like the persimmon, were grafted on to other cultures—China, Tibet, Korea, Japan… and now in the West where, "the sweet persimmon is being nurtured…" Uchiyama's wish is that we should all become sweet persimmons, "bearing the sweet fruit of a compassionate life…."

With an hour or so before the next bus, we celebrated the completion of our pilgrimage with a bowl of matcha and an autumn wagashi. The tea served in this nondescript café along the pathway to Kegonji was not in the formal style with expensive bowls and elegant equipment, but a bowl of tea served on a plain tray: simple and ordinary. We savored our sweet, drank the bright green froth, and let the satisfied feeling of completion seep into our very being.

Epilogue

When we returned to Kyoto, Gwen flew back to the States ahead of me to attend her second training in animal healing. I stayed on for a few days to take some ikebana classes. With extra time on my hands I thought it would be interesting to revisit some of the pilgrimage temples in the city to have one last look, take some more photos, and relive some of the highlights of our journey. Maybe the elderly nun would remember me, shake my hand again, impart another blessing.

I entered the Kodo compound from Teramachi Street just as before. The flowers in the temizuya vases looked fresh as before; colorful flags representing the five esoteric healing energies flapped in the breeze; the smiling face of Benzaiten appeared through an opening in the flags. As before, the temple steward sat in the temple office waiting for her next pilgrim. But the elderly nun wasn't sitting beside her. Was she out for the day? Ill? Had she passed away? I didn't inquire. I didn't want to know.

I would soon discover that outside the context of pilgrimage an element of... was it sacredness, was missing. The spectacular Amida Buddha in the meditation hall at Kiyomizudera had been removed; the transformational "birth canal" tunnel honoring Daizuigu Bodhisattva was closed; Kannonji, festive and full of life on our first visit, was now nearly deserted; the friendly monk at Rokuharamitsuji was gone.

There is a well-known saying in Japan: *Ichi-go, ichi-e*, which means "one time, one encounter," or "one chance in a lifetime." It was the scroll on the wall of our *tatami* room at Tenruji, a temple that serves the special *shojin ryori* vegetarian cuisine where Gwen and I had our "pilgrimage completion" celebration.

On pilgrimage my intention had been one of wanting to experience the essence of the divine feminine: the Buddha of Compassion, and to travel the path that thousands had trod for centuries. Many experiences along the way, like the nun at Kodo, felt extraordinary, a kind of pilgrim's blessing. It, like so many other encounters, had been ichi-go, ichi-e.

Disappointed that I wouldn't see the nun again, I left Kodo with the memory of her blessing. I continued down Teramachi Street, past the antique shop, the handmade paper shop, the famous tea shop, and headed for the French bakery. Outside of pilgrimage and the power of a higher intention, it was just another ordinary day in Kyoto.

Directions to the 33 Temples of Kannon

(Directions are from Kyoto Station unless otherwise noted.)

(The HyperDia website gives various times and train routes to all destinations within Japan, as does Jorudan.)

Seigantoji – Temple #1: At Kyoto Station, reserve a seat on the Kuroshio (rapid train) for Kii-Katsura. (Limited schedule, check in advance.) At Kii-Katsura Station take a bus to the village of Nachi-san. The bus takes about 30-40 minutes and runs fairly regularly. Plan to stay overnight, especially if you want to continue on to Temple 2, 3 and 4. Try a small ryokan called Mitaki Sanso, reserved through Kumano Travel.

Kimiidera – Temple #2: Best reached in conjunction with Seigantoji (Temple 1), otherwise another long train ride to Wakayama City. From Seigantoji return to Kii-Katsura Station and take an express train on the JR Kisei Line to Wakayama Station. Transfer to a local train on the same line. Get off at Kimiidera Station. The temple is a short walk south of the station (taxi optional).

Kokawadera – Temple #3: Best reached in conjunction with Kimiidera (Temple 2) and Seigantoji (Temple 1). From Kimiidera take a JR local train on the Kisei Line to Wakayama City. Change to the JR Wakayama Line local to Kokawa. The temple is a 10-15 minute walk north of Kokawa Station.

Sefukuji (Makinoodera) – Temple #4: From Wakayama Station take a JR local on the Hanwa Line to Izumi Fucho. The temple is about 10 miles from the station. Buses run infrequently and take an hour. A taxi might be a better option. The hike up the mountain is steep and takes 30-40 minutes.

Fujidera – Temple #5: From Kyoto Station take the JR to Tennoji Station in Osaka. Transfer to the Kintetsu Osaka Line and get off at Fujidera Station. The temple is a two-minute walk through a shopping arcade.

Tsubosakadera – Temple #6: At Kyoto Station purchase a reserved seat on a Kintetsu Limited Express bound for Kashiharajingue-mae. Once arrived, transfer to a local train and get off at Tsubosakayama Station. Take a bus from the train station to Tsubosakadera. Buses run frequently and stop in front of the temple. Taxis are also available.

Okadrea – Temple #7: Easiest if coupled with a visit to Tsubosakadera (Temple 6) on the same day; otherwise, you have to purchase another expensive reserved ticket on the Kintetsu Limited Express. From Tsubosakayama Station take a local on the Kintetsu Yoshino Line to Okadera Station. Take a bus to the foot of the hill by the temple. From the bus stop, Okadera is a ten-minute walk (a taxi is optional).

Hasedera – Temple #8: From Kyoto Station take the Kintetsu Line to Yamato-yagi Station. Change for Hasedera Station. The temple is a 15-minute walk from the station. The route is not direct. Ask for directions or take a taxi.

Nan'endo – Temple #9: For the direct route, take the Kintetsu train from Kyoto and get off at Nara Station. You can walk to the Kofukuji complex and Nan'endo from the train station. From the JR train, take a bus or taxi to Kofukuji complex.

Mimurotoji – Temple #10: From Kyoto Station take the Keihan Main Line to Chushojima. Change to the Uji Line and get off at Mimurodo. The temple is a 20-minute walk from the station, across the river. Go to Uji Station if you want a bus.

Kami Daigoji - Temple #11: From Kyoto City take the Tozei Subway Line to Daigo Station; then a bus or taxi to Daigoji, the lower temple complex. You can access the Upper (Kami) Daigoji trail by purchasing two entrance tickets: one for the Lower Daigo temple (a must see and the place where you'll get your pilgrim stamp), and the other to exit Lower Daigo through a turnstile that leads to the Upper Daigo complex.

You can also access the trail before the entrance to Lower

Daigoji. Turn right to find the path that runs parallel to the temple complex fence. (There's a restroom along this section, and the only one you'll encounter on the trail.) Continue on along this path until it turns into a staircase leading up the mountain. Follow this staircase all the way to the top. The hike up takes over an hour, depending on your level of fitness and speed; and the hike down also takes about an hour. There's a guide rope that runs along the center of the stairs that comes in handy, especially on the way down, as it is steep and the stairs are uneven. For more information on Daigoji visit their website.

Iwamadera - Temple #12: From JR Kyoto Station, take the JR Biwako Line for Yasu and get off at Ishiyama Station. At Ishiyama Station change to the Keihan Ishiyama-Sakamoto Line (follow signs up the stairs) and get off at Ishiyamadera Station. Walk 10 minutes to Ishiyamadera (Temple 13) to find a taxi. The taxi will cost about 3,800 yen (2012 prices). On the way back from Iwamadera (Temple 12) you should have time to visit Ishiyamadera before heading back to Kyoto.

Ishiyamadera – Temple #13: From Kyoto Station take the JR Biwako Line to Ishiyama Station. Change to the Keihan Line and take a local to Ishiyamadera Station. The temple is a 10-minute walk down the main boulevard outside the station.

Miidera – Temple #14: Best if done the same day as Iwamadera (Temple 12) and/or Ishiyamadera (Temple 13). From Ishiyamadera Station take the Keihan Line to Miidera. The temple is a 10-to 15-minute walk. Ask for directions, or take a taxi.

Imakumano Kannonji – Temple #15: This temple is in the Senyuji-Tofukuji temple compound in Kyoto City. From Kyoto Station take a JR Uji Line to Tofukuji Station or a bus from a convenient Kyoto location. The temple is a 15-minute walk from the station. Walk under a bridge and look for signs.

Kiyomizudera - Temple #16: This temple is in Kyoto City. From JR Kyoto Station take a Bus #202 or #100 to Gojo-zaka or

Kiyomizu-michi. Follow the crowd up the hill. **Rokuharamitsuji – Temple #17**: This temple is in Kyoto City. Visit on the same day as Kiyomizudera (Temple 16); it is a 10-minute walk in the opposite direction from the main starting point (Higashi-dori). Walk down Kakimachi. The temple is on the right.

Rokkakudo – Temple #18: This temple is in Kyoto City. It is located off of Karasuma-dori, between Oike-dori and Shijo-dori, a short walk from Karasuma Station on the Hankyu Kyoto Line, or subway. You enter from a side street or through the Starbucks on Karasuma.

Kodo – Temple #19: This temple is in Kyoto City, a short walk from the Imperial Palace, and right off of Teramachi-dori on the west side of the street.

Yoshiminedera – Temple #20: From Kyoto Station take a local train on the JR Tokaido Line to Mukomachi Station; then a bus #66 at bus stop #2 in front of the west exit of the train station. Buses leave every hour and take about 30 minutes. The bus stop is about a 10-minute walk from the temple entrance up a very steep hill. A taxi is optional from Mukomachi Station; it goes to the temple entrance.

Anaoji – Temple #21: From Kyoto Station (or Enmachi Station) take a local on the JR San'in Line for Kameoka Station. From the station take a bus #34 or #59; the bus leaves every hour. The bus passes Anaoji and stops at a turn-around about a block away. The return bus arrives at 19 minutes past the hour (check schedule for current times).

Sojiji – Temple #22: Go to the Hankyu Train Station (Shijo-Kawaramachi in Kyoto) and take a Limited Express to Takatsukishi. Transfer to a local train and get off at Sojiji Station. Go out the Central Exit. (There is a map of the area by the exit.) Take a soft right. Walk about 1 block and turn right again. The temple is at the end of the street.

Katsuoji – Temple #23: From Kyoto Hankyu Train Station (Shijo-Kawaramachi) take a Limited Express to Ibarakishi. At

Ibarakishi transfer to a local and get off at Minami-Ibaraki. At Minami-Ibaraki transfer to the Osaka Monorail and get off at Senri-chuo. At Senri-chuo Station take bus #29 (far end of the bus terminal to the left). There are very few buses, but the bus stops directly in front of the temple. Check the schedule at the bus stop as there are very few return times.

Nakayamadera – Temple #24: Best to do Temple 23 and 24 on the same day. Take the train from Senri-chuo Station to Hotarugaike. Change to the Hankyu Train and get off at Nakayama Station. If leaving from Kyoto take the Hankyu Train to Nakayama Station. The temple is a 2-minute walk.

Kiyomizudera – Temple #25: From Kyoto Station take a Special Rapid train on the Tokaido-Sanyo Line to Amagasaki. Change to the Tambaji-Rapid train on the Fukuchiyama Line and get off at Aino. Take the Shinki bus to Kiyomizudera (there are only two going and two returning); the bus stops directly in front of the temple, or you can get off at the base of the mountain and walk up the old pilgrim's path. (The bus passes through the famous pottery town and ancient kiln site of Tachikui, home of Tamba-yaki (ceramic ware). If you have time, you can make a stop here and catch the last bus back to Aino. The bus driver will drop you in the village and pick you up at The Museum of Ceramic Art farther up the hill.)

Ichijoji – Temple #26: From Kyoto Station take a Special Rapid or an even faster Hikari train to Himeji. Go out the North exit of Himeji Station. To the left is the Shinki Bus Terminal. Buy a round trip ticket at the ticket counter for Hokkezan-Ichijoji (Bus #71). Wait in line inside the bus terminal until the bus number is called. The bus takes about 35 minutes and has a limited schedule; it drops you directly in front of Ichijoji.

Engyoji – Temple #27: Same route to Himeji and the Shinki Bus Terminal as Temple 26. Buy a round trip ticket for bus #8 and the Shoshazan Ropeway. At the bus stop follow the signs to the ropeway. The ride up the mountain takes about 5 minutes. From the ropeway at the top of the mountain, you can take a mini-van to the temple compound for an extra fee, or walk up the old pilgrim's path (a fairly easy walk at about 10 minutes). Engyoji provides overnight accommodations and special vegetarian meals (shun-s-k [shun-s-k@shosha.or.jp].)

Nariaiji – Temple #28: From Kyoto Station take a Special Rapid train to Amanohashidate. Inside Amanohashidate Station pick up a map and buy a round trip ticket to Nariaiji from the Information Table. Follow the instructions to the water taxi (a 5-minute walk through town). Board a water taxi and cross the Asokai lagoon. From the boat dock, cross the street and walk through a Shinto shrine to the cable car station. The cable car takes about 5 minutes. (For those who like a more thrilling ride, you have the option of riding up in an open ski-lift type of chair.) At the top of the mountain board a bus for the temple (about a 10-minute ride). You can stay on the bus to the temple parking lot, or get off lower down at the Niomon and walk up (very short, easy walk).

Matsuno-odera – Temple #29: From Temple 28 take a train from Amanohashidate to Higashi-Maizuru, or from Kyoto Station take a Special-Rapid train to Higashi-Maizuru; then arrange a taxi (2 hour minimum) to take you to Matsuno-odera, or take a local train to Matsuno-odera Station and walk about 50 minutes to the temple. There are no buses to the temple.

Hogonji – Temple #30: Hogonji is located on Chikubushima (Chikubu Island) in the middle of Lake Biwa. From Kyoto Station, take a Special Rapid train on the Kosei Line for the port of Omi-Imazu. Stop at the tourist shop in the station and get a 10% discount card for the boat. Exit the train station and walk approximately two blocks toward the lake and the boat dock. Buy a round-trip ticket to Chikubushima and pay attention to the return time. There are four boats per day, seven days a week between March 15 and December 6 (9:40; 10:50; 12:00 and 13:10). Check for current updates.

Chomeiji – Temple #31: From Kyoto Station take a train on the Tokaido-Sanyo Line directly to Omi-Hachiman (approx. 43 mins.). From Omi-Hachiman take the #6 bus to Chomeiji, which is the last stop. Cross over the road from the bus stop to find the 808 steps that lead to the temple. An alternative route is to walk the road or take a taxi to the upper parking lot. There are still several steep stairs to get to the temple compound from the parking lot. The return trip is easier via the road.

Kannonshoji – Temple #32: From Kyoto Station take a train on the Tokaido-Sanyo Line to Notogawa Station (approx. 51 minutes). From the train station I recommend taking a taxi. Pay the toll gate fee and continue to the parking lot. The temple is about a 15-minute walk from the parking lot. Have the taxi wait.

Kegonji – Temple #33: From Kyoto Station take a Special Rapid on the Tokaido-Sanyo Line to Maibara. At Maibara change to the JR Tokai line for Ogaki. At Ogaki find the one-car train on the Tarumi Tetsudo line to Tanigumiguchi. Buy your train ticket at the booth on the track. At Tanigumiguchi a bus takes you to the temple. There are only five going and six coming back. Check the times.

Glossary of Terms

Amida Buddha: (Sanskrit: Amitabha) known as the Buddha of Infinite Light and Life in Pure Land Buddhism.

Avalokitesvara: a Sanskrit name for the Bodhisattva of Compassion who is portrayed as either male or female depending on the culture. In Japan Avalokitesvara is known as Kannon; in China as Guanyin; in Tibet as Chenrezig.

bardo: a Tibetan word meaning "intermediate state" in general, but often thought of as the state between death and rebirth.

Benzaiten: (Sanskrit: Saraswati) a Japanese Buddhist deity who appears in the *Lotus Sutra* and the *Sutra of Golden Light*. Found in Buddhist and Shinto traditions, she presides over everything that flows, including water, poetry, eloquent speech, music and knowledge.

bodhisattva: a Sanskrit term used in the Mahayana tradition for those who have generated a spontaneous wish to attain Buddhahood for the benefit of all sentient beings; a bodhisattva foregoes entering nirvana in order to help others who are not yet liberated; the term has entered colloquial vocabulary as an expression for anyone who bestows kindness upon others.

chabana: an ikebana flower arrangement with its own style and rules used exclusively in the tea ceremony.

Chado: the Japanese tea ceremony, or Way of Tea, a spiritual and aesthetic discipline for refinement of the self.

Daizuigu Bodhisattva: (Sanskrit: Mahapratisara) deity found in the Mahayana and Vajrayana traditions, and honored in particular at Kiyomizudera, Temple 16.

engi: a narrative historical account that chronicles the founding story of a Buddhist temple or Shinto shrine.

En no Gyoja: a mystical ascetic of the 7th century who founded Shugendo, a syncretic religion still practiced in remote mountains of Japan.

ema: a small wooden plaque often with an animal motif from the Asian Zodiac; Shinto shrine visitors inscribe a wish or prayer on the back of the ema, and then hang it where kami or spirits can receive it.

gaijin: literally means "outside person," but is generally used to describe a foreigner or non-Japanese.

goeika: a sacred and symbolic poem written in the traditional tanka form of 5-7-5-7-7 syllables and chanted at a temple to invoke the spirit of a Buddha or bodhisattva such as Kannon.

hondo: the main hall in Japanese Buddhist temple compounds which enshrines the principle deity of veneration.

irimoya: a hip-and-gable roof design imported from China and used in Buddhist temples and Shinto shrines in Japan.

Izumi Shikibu: one of the Thirty-six Medieval Poetry Immortals; she is considered to be the greatest woman poet of the Heian period.

Jizo Bodhisattva: (Sanskrit: Ksitigarbha) one of the most venerated deities in Japan. In particular he is a bodhisattva and guardian of children and aborted fetuses, but has vowed to help all beings in the "six realms." In Japan he is often depicted as a childlike deity wearing hats and bibs, but can also be represented as a monk.

Karana mudra: a hand gesture meant to ward off evil or negativity; performed by turning palm forward, pressing down on the two middle fingers with the thumb, and extending index and little finger straight up.

kami: the spiritual force or divine energy existing in all aspects of nature, including humans.

Kannon: (Sanskrit: Avalokitesvara; Chinese: Guanyin.) Also known in Japan as Kanzeon and Kannon-sama and depicted as male or female, he/she is "One Who Hears the Cries of the World." According to the *Lotus Sutra* Kannon has 33 manifestations; thus the 33 Kannon pilgrimage temples.

ki: the word can mean many things in Japanese, but is most often referred to in the Reiki healing tradition as "spiritual energy."

Kobo Daishi: posthumous name for the Buddhist monk Kukai (774-835), founder of Shingon Buddhism, the temple city of Koyasan, and the 88 Temple Pilgrimage of Shikoku.

Kumano Kodo: a network of ancient pilgrimage routes that crisscross the Kii Peninsula in the southern Kansai region of Japan; the area was designated a UNESCO World Heritage site in 2004.

Maitreya: the bodhisattva who will appear as the future Buddha when Buddhism will have been forgotten; he will achieve enlightenment and teach the pure dharma to sentient beings much like Buddha Shakyamuni did.

Mara: the demon who tempted Buddha with power, beautiful women and anything that would dissuade him from attaining enlightenment; mara is also a metaphor for anything that tempts or triggers desirous attachments.

matcha: powdered green tea traditionally used in Chado, the Japanese tea ceremony; it is whisked with a bamboo whisk until frothy and served in special tea bowls.

Mizuko Jizo: the bodhisattva who looks after "water babies," or stillborn, aborted and miscarried fetuses; numerous Mizuko Jizo statues wearing hats and bibs can be found at most Buddhist temples in Japan.

mottainai: a Japanese expression of regret for wasting anything precious such as food, water or resources; it roughly means, "What a waste!" or "Don't waste."

Nio: two wrathful, muscular guardians of the Buddha and the dharma found at the entrance of most Buddhist temples in Japan.

nokyo: office where one receives the "pilgrim's stamp" or nokyocho.

nokyocho: a temple stamp placed in the pilgrim's book, indicating the temple's name and date of the pilgrim's visit.

noren: fabric dividers or curtains cut into long vertical strips and hung in windows or doorways.

osetai: a gift of any kind given to a pilgrim; the act of generosity has the added benefit of creating positive karma.

Sakuteiki: "Records of Garden Making," a traditional garden text book that defines the art of landscape gardening as an aesthetic endeavor based on poetic feeling of the designer and the site; it taught that the placement of stones was considered the most important part of the garden design.

samsara: a Sanskrit word that indicates the cycle of wandering in ignorance through the six realms of existence.

senbazuru: a string of 1,000 paper origami cranes; an ancient legend promises that anyone who folds 1,000 cranes will be granted a wish by the gods.

shaktipat: a Sanskrit word meaning "psychic energy"; a kind of grace that can be transmitted from a holy person to a disciple through a look, touch, word, flower or fruit.

shimenawa: "enclosing rope" used in the Shinto religion for ritual purification and to denote spiritual presence around sacred objects, such as trees and rocks.

Shingon Buddhism: Japanese esoteric Buddhism, a Vajrayana lineage brought to Japan from China in the 9th century by the monk Kukai (Kobo Daishi).

Shinto: means "way of the kami" and refers to the native spiritual philosophy of Japan, a belief in the divinity or the sacred essence found in all forms of nature, including humans, rocks, trees, rivers, etc.; this "sacred essence" or "kami" permeates all things.

Shodo: the Way of Calligraphy, a meditative and artistic writing practice using ink and handmade papers.

shojin ryori: or "devotion cuisine," a Buddhist vegetarian or vegan cuisine based on the philosophy of *ahimsa*, or non-violence.

skillful means: a term taken from the chapter "Skillful Means" in *The Lotus Sutra* to denote how a Buddha or bodhisattva, through their wisdom eye, will use whatever necessary to teach the dharma, or show the way, according to each person's need or ability.

temizuya: a water-filled basin used at Shinto-Buddhist shrines for ritual purification.

Tendai Buddhism: a Mahayana sect brought to Japan from China in the 8th century by the monk Saicho; it became established at Enryaku-ji on Mt. Hiei near Kyoto.

tokanoma: an alcove in a traditional Japanese room where artistic items such as an ikebana arrangement, poetic scroll, incense burner or candle holder are displayed.

Ultimate Truth: from the Two Truths doctrine (Ultimate and Relative) of the Madhyamaka School founded by Nagarjuna, who proclaimed that ordinary experience and conceptual thought are elusive or "empty."

Vajrayana Buddhism: a Buddhist view that signifies the real and indestructible essence of a human being versus the fictionalized narrative an individual entertains; an esoteric philosophy and practice utilizing mudras, mandalas and mantras.

wagashi: traditional and often symbolic Japanese confections served with matcha (whisked green tea).

yamabushi: Japanese mountain ascetics who follow Shugendo.

zazen: literally means "seated meditation," a practice used to gain insight into the nature of existence.

References

Books

Bodhi, Bhikkhu (editor). *In the Buddha's Words: An Anthology of Discourses from the Pali Canon.* Boston: Wisdom Publications, 2005.

Blofeld, John. *Bodhisattva of Compassion: the Mystical Tradition of Kuan Yin.* Boston: Shambhala, 2009.

Brunnhölzl, Karl. *The Heart Attack Sutra: A New Commentary on the Heart Sutra.* Ithaca: Snow Lion Publications, 2012.

Cousineau, Phil. *The Art of Pilgrimage: The Seeker's Guide to Making Travel Sacred.* San Francisco: Conari Press, 1998.

Harada Roshi, Shodo. *Zazen Wasan, Song of Zazen.* Tahoma Zen Monastery, One Drop Zen, 2017.

McTaggart, Lynne. *The Field: The Quest for the Secret Force of the Universe.* New York: HarperCollins, 2008.

Palmer, Martin and Jay Ramsay with Man-Ho Kwok. *Kuan Yin: Myths and Prophecies of the Chinese Goddess of Compassion.* London: Thorsons, 1995.

Pye, Michael. *Japanese Buddhist Pilgrimage.* Sheffield: Equinox, 2015.

Readicker-Henderson, Ed. *The Traveler's Guide to Japanese Pilgrimages.* New York: Weatherhill, 1995.

Reeves, Gene (translation and introduction). *The Lotus Sutra: a Contemporary Translation of a Buddhist Classic.* Boston: Wisdom Publications, 2008.

Stiene, Frans. *The Inner Heart of Reiki: Rediscovering Your True Self.* Winchester, UK: Ayni Books, 2015.

Teneda, Santoka. *Mountain Tasting: Haiku and Journals of Santoka Teneda.* (Translated and introduced by John Stevens.) Buffalo: White Pine Press, 2009.

Tyler, Royall (editor & translator). *Japanese Nō Dramas.* Penguin Books, 1992.

Uchiyama, Kosho. *Opening the Hand of Thought*. (Translated and edited by Tom Wright, Jisho Warner & Shohaku Okumura). Boston: Wisdom Publications, 2004.

Victoria, Brian Daizen. *Zen at War* (second edition). Lanham: Rowman & Littlefield Publishers, Inc., 2006.

Yamasaki, Taikō. *Shingon: Japanese Esoteric Buddhism*. (Translated by Richard Peterson and Cynthia Peterson; edited by Yasuyoshi Morimoto and David Kidd.) Boston: Shambhala, 1988.

Periodicals

Endo, Yoshiko (text); Katsuhiko Mizuno and Akira Takemae (photography); Kyoko Tsukada, Junko Maejima and Tomoyuki Kusaka (contributions). "50 Temples and Their Flowers: A Pilgrimage." `Kateigaho International Edition*. Vol. 25. Spring/Summer 2010.

Websites

Juno, Kate Kodo. "Saigoku Kannon Pilgrimage." http://sacredjapan.com/. Copyright © 2009.

Bibliography

Books

Bays, Jan Chozen. Jizo Bodhisattva: *Modern Healing & Traditional Buddhist Practice.* Boston: Tuttle Publishing, 2002.

Clift, Jean Dalby & Wallace B. Clift. *The Archetype of Pilgrimage.* New York: Paulist Press, 1996.

Dougill, John. *Japan's World Heritage Sites.* Tokyo: Tuttle, 2014.

Ehrlich, Gretel. *Facing the Wave: A Journey in the Wake of the Tsunami.* New York: Vintage Books, 2013.

Ferguson, Andy. *Tracking Bodhidharma: A Journey to the Heart of Chinese Culture.* Berkley: Counterpoint, 2012.

Goddard, Dwight. *The Buddha's Golden Path: The Classic Introduction to Zen Buddhism.* New York: Square One Publishers, 2002.

Leighton, Taigen Dan. *Faces of Compassion: Classic Bodhisattva Archetypes and Their Modern Expression.* Boston: Wisdom Publications, 2012.

Lipton, Bruce H. *The Biology of Belief: Unleashing the Power of Consciousness, Matter & Miracle.* Santa Rosa: Mountain of Love/Elite Books, 2005.

Lopez, Donald S. Jr. *The Story of Buddhism.* New York: HarperCollins, 2001.

Martin, Rafe. *Endless Path: Awakening Within the Buddhist Imagination: Jataka Tales, Zen Practice, and Daily Life.* Berkeley: North Atlantic Books, 2010.

Murasaki, Shikibu. *The Tale of Genji.* (Translated and abridged by Edward G. Seidensticker.) New York: Vintage Classics, a Division of Random House, Inc., 1976 (1990 edition).

Reader, Ian. *Making Pilgrimages: Meaning and Practice in Shikoku.* Honolulu: University of Hawai'i Press, 2005.

Red Pine (translator). *The Zen Teaching of Bodhidharma.* New York: North Point Press (Farrar, Straus and Giroux), 1987.

Renard, John. *101 Questions and Answers on Buddhism*. New York: Gramercy Books, 1999.

Rockwell, Irini Nadel. *The Five Wisdom Energies: A Buddhist Way of Understanding Personalities, Emotions, and Relationships*. Boston: Shambhala, 2002.

Schireson, Grace. *Zen Women: Beyond Tea Ladies, Iron Maidens and Macho Masters*. Boston: Wisdom Publications, 2009.

Shaw, Sarah. *The Jatakas: Birth Stories of the Bodhisattva*. New Delhi: Penguin Books, 2006.

Sibley, Robert C. *The Way of the 88 Temples: Journeys on the Shikoku Pilgrimage*. Charlottesville: University of Virginia Press, 2013.

Tanabe, George J. (editor). *Religions of Japan in Practice*. Princeton University Press, 1999.

Watsky, Andrew Mark. *Chikubushima: Deploying the Sacred Arts in Momoyama Japan*. Seattle: University of Washington Press, 2004.

Periodicals

Kimbrough, R. Keller. "Reading the Miraculous Powers of Japanese Poetry: Spells, Truth Acts, and a Medieval Buddhist Poetics of the Supernatural." *Japanese Journal of Religious Studies* 32/1: 1-33. Nanzan Institute of Religion and Culture, 2005.

MacWilliams, Mark. "Living Icons: *Reizo* Myths of the Saikoku Kannon Pilgrimage." *History of Religions*, Vol. 34, No. 4. Monumenta Nipponica, Sophia University. May, 1995.

Tulku Rinpoche, Tara. "A New Dwelling." *Parabola*, Vol: 9.3 *Pilgrimage*. Reprinted by Morning Light Press, 2005.

Films

Abela, Jean-Marc and McGuire, Mark Patrick. *Shugendo Now*. Festival Media, 2012.

Websites

Emmott, Craig. "The Saigoku Kannon Pilgrimage." http://www. taleofgenji.org/saigoku_pilgrimage.html. Copyright © 2001-2015_

Schumacher, Mark. "Kannon Notebook." http://www.onmark productions.com/html/kannon.shtml. Copyright © 1995-2014

About the Author

Joan Diane Stamm was born in 1952 in Langdon, North Dakota. She grew up in a rural community of wheat farmers. Nothing in her upbringing foretold of a later interest in Japan and Japanese culture, but in 1970, while a student at Western Washington University, an interest in Eastern philosophy developed. She took a meditative yoga class and began reading books like *The Way of* Zen by Alan Watts. Not until 1991, when she followed her sister to Japan to teach English would she participate in her first Zen experience at a training temple in Kobe. An interest in Buddhism deepened during the two years she lived in Japan, and continued upon her return home to Seattle, Washington. In 1993 she began what would be a lifelong study and practice of Zen and Tibetan Buddhism, as well as *ikebana* (the art of Japanese flower arranging). Ikebana, coupled with Buddhist practice, led to her first book on Japanese culture, *Heaven and Earth are Flowers: Reflections on Ikebana and Buddhism*, a Nautilus Book Award winner. (Nautilus recognizes books that make a "spiritual contribution for a better world.")

After many trips to Japan to study ikebana, and many years studying and practicing Buddhism with a variety of notable teachers, the idea of a Buddhist pilgrimage was born. In 2012, the year she turned 60, she embarked on the Saigoku Kannon Pilgrimage of 33 Temples; that same year she co-founded Cold Mountain Hermitage, a Buddhist study and practice group on Orcas Island where she lives.

In addition to Stamm's training in meditation and Buddhism, she holds an MFA in writing and literature from Bennington College, and a BA in Art from the Evergreen State College. For more information, please visit her website at www.JoanDStamm.com.

MANTRA
BOOKS

MANTRA BOOKS

EASTERN RELIGION & PHILOSOPHY

We publish books on Eastern religions and philosophies. Books that aim to inform and explore the various traditions that began in the East and have migrated West.
If you have enjoyed this book, why not tell other readers by posting a review on your preferred book site. Recent bestsellers from MANTRA BOOKS are:

The Way Things Are
A Living Approach to Buddhism
Lama Ole Nydahl
An introduction to the teachings of the Buddha, and how to make use of these teachings in everyday life.
Paperback: 978-1-84694-042-2 ebook: 978-1-78099-845-9

Back to the Truth
5000 Years of Advaita
Dennis Waite
A demystifying guide to Advaita for both those new to, and those familiar with this ancient, non-dualist philosophy from India.
Paperback: 978-1-90504-761-1 ebook: 978-184694-624-0

In the Light of Meditation

Mike George

A comprehensive introduction to the practice of meditation and the spiritual principles behind it. A 10 lesson meditation programme with CD and internet support.

Paperback: 978-1-90381-661-5

Less Dust the More Trust

The Participating in The Shamatha Project, Meditation and Science

Adeline van Waning, MD PhD

The inside-story of a woman participating in frontline meditation research, exploring the interfaces of mind-practice, science and psychology.

Paperback: 978-1-78099-948-7 ebook: 978-1-78279-657-2

I Know How To Live, I Know How To Die

The Teachings of Dadi Janki: A warm, radical, and life-affirming view of who we are, where we come from, and what time is calling us to do

Neville Hodgkinson

Life and death are explored in the context of frontier science and deep soul awareness.

Paperback: 978-1-78535-013-9 ebook: 978-1-78535-014-6

Living Jainism

An Ethical Science

Aidan Rankin, Kanti V. Mardia

A radical new perspective on science rooted in intuitive awareness and deductive reasoning.

Paperback: 978-1-78099-912-8 ebook: 978-1-78099-911-1

A Path of Joy
Popping into Freedom
Paramananda Ishaya
A simple and joyful path to spiritual enlightenment.
Paperback: 978-1-78279-323-6 ebook: 978-1-78279-322-9

Ordinary Women, Extraordinary Wisdom
The Feminine Face of Awakening
Rita Marie Robinson
A collection of intimate conversations with female spiritual
teachers who live like ordinary women, but are engaged with their
true natures.
Paperback: 978-1-84694-068-2 ebook: 978-1-78099-908-1

Shinto
A celebration of Life
Aidan Rankin
Introducing a gentle but powerful spiritual pathway reconnecting
humanity with Great Nature and affirming all aspects of life.
Paperback: 978-1-84694-438-3 ebook: 978-1-84694-738-4

The Way of Nothing
The Nothing in the Way
Paramananda Ishaya
A fresh and light-hearted exploration of the amazing reality of
nothingness.
Paperback: 978-1-78279-307-6 ebook: 978-1-78099-840-4

Readers of ebooks can buy or view any of these bestsellers by clicking on the live link in the title. Most titles are published in paperback and as an ebook. Paperbacks are available in traditional bookshops. Both print and ebook formats are available online.

Find more titles and sign up to our readers' newsletter at http://www.johnhuntpublishing.com/mind-body-spirit. Follow us on Facebook at https://www.facebook.com/OBooks and Twitter at https://twitter.com/obooks.